An Introduction to Building Applications with Blazor

How to get started creating applications using this exciting easy to use Microsoft C# framework

Michael Washington

www.BlazorHelpWebsite.com

An Introduction to Building Applications with Blazor

How to get started creating applications using this exciting easy to use Microsoft C# framework

Copyright September 2019
Published By
Blazor Help Website

BlazorHelpWebsite.com

Copyright

Proofreading by Peter J. Francis,
hgpublishing@gmail.com
www.hgpublishing.com

Special Thanks

Microsoft

Steve Sanderson

Daniel Roth

Ryan Nowak

Anthony Chu

David Fowler

Eilon Lipton

Javier Calvarro Nelson

Pranav K

Artak

N. Taylor Mullen

Ajay Bhargav Baaskaran

Blazor Community

Shaun Walker

Chris Sainty

Ed Charbeneau

$\mathcal{M}$ister$\mathcal{M}$agoo

Atanas Korchev

Vladimir Enchev

Vladimir Samoilenko

Peter Leslie Morris

Vakhtangi Abashidze

Steven T. Cramer

Dani Herrera

Karl Shifflett

Shahed Chowdhuri

Henry Alberto Rodriguez

Michael Luna

David Masterson

Sean Moran

Table of Contents

An Introduction to Building Applications with Blazor 1

Copyright...3

Special Thanks..4

   Microsoft 4

   Blazor Community 4

Table of Contents 6

Dedication..10

Preface 11

     Requirements 11

Chapter 1: What is Blazor?...12

     Disadvantage: 13

     Advantages: 13

   Different Modes of Blazor...14

   Blazor Features 15

     Components..16

     Data Binding..17

     Routing 22

     Forms and Validation 24

     JavaScript Interop..25

Chapter 2: Getting Started..27

   Create the Default Project 28

   Explore the Default Application...32

Examine the Project Files 37

Routing and Layouts...39

Dependency Injection 42

Chapter 3: Blazor Binding, Events and Parameters 48

Create the Page 49

One Way Binding..54

Two Way Binding 56

Create a To Do Page...60

Parameters 72

Calling a Method on a Child Component..77

Events 81

Cascading Parameters...85

Chapter 4: Creating a Step-By-Step End-To-End Database Server-Side Blazor Application 93

Use SQL Server..94

Create the Blazor Application 95

Create the Database 101

Add a Table to the Database..112

Create the Data Context..118

Read from the Database...129

Inserting Data into the Database..138

Updating the Data...146

Deleting the Data..155

Chapter 5: Blazor Forms and Validation...163

Add Data Annotations 165

Add the Form Validation Controls 168

Validate a Dropdown Control 177

Customizing Validation...180

Chapter 6: Implementing State Management in Blazor 185

The Issue – State Is Not Maintained...186

Implementing State Management..192

Advanced State Management Using EventCallback 199

Consume the Updated State Management Class 205

Chapter 7: Creating Blazor Templated Components............................211

Create the Dialog Control...215

Create the Templated Component 224

Creating a Generic Templated Component 232

Chapter 8: Blazor JavaScript Interop 240

Starting With State Manager 240

Using JavaScript Interop 243

From JavaScript Back to Blazor with Parameters.........................251

Using ElementReference and the @ref Attribute...........................258

Blazor State Management Using Local Storage.............................267

Chapter 9: A Demonstration of Simple Server-Side Blazor Cookie Authentication 279

Application Authentication 280

Create the Application...281

Add Nuget Packages...283

Add Cookie Authentication...284

Add Login/Logout Pages...288

Login.cshtml...289

Login.cshtml.cs...289

Logout.cshtml 291

Logout.cshtml.cs 291

Add Client Code 293

Calling Server Side Controller Methods 299

Chapter 10: Deploying a Server Side Blazor Application To Azure 308

Create the Blazor Application 309

Publish to Azure 313

Create SignalR Service 323

Add SignalR Service 328

Using User Secrets 332

About the Author 337

Dedication

As always, for Valerie and Zachary.

Preface

Requirements

To implement the example code, the following are required:

- **Microsoft Windows 7 Service Pac 1** (or higher) or **Microsoft Windows Server 2012 R2 Service Pac 1** (or higher)
- **Visual Studio 2019 Version 16.3** (or higher) (Free download from: https://visualstudio.microsoft.com/free-developer-offers/)
- **SQL Server 2017 Developer Edition** (or higher) (Free download from: https://www.microsoft.com/en-us/sql-server/sql-server-downloads)

Chapter 1: What is Blazor?

Microsoft's Blazor is a framework for building **rich interactive web applications**.

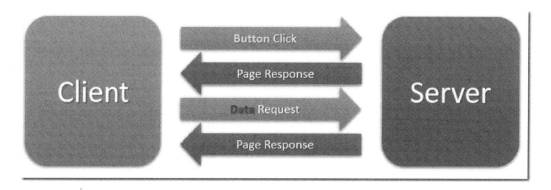

In a **non-interactive web application**, all interaction from the client (the web browser) requires *events* (like *button clicks*) and data to be *communicated* to the **server,** and the entire web page has to be *reloaded* to process the *response*.

Disadvantage:

- **Slower** – the page is repainted on each interaction

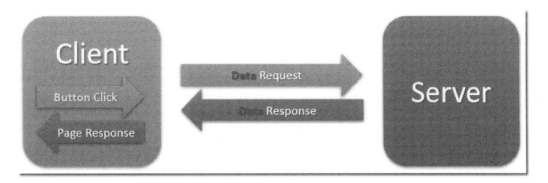

In an interactive web application, only an interaction from the client that requires data from the server needs to be communicated to the server, and the entire web page <u>does not</u> need to be reloaded to process the response, only the required portions of the web page.

Advantages:

- **Faster** - The page is <u>not</u> repainted on each interaction
- Until **Blazor**, this required an additional language such as **JavaScript** or **TypeScript** (that created JavaScript).

Note: **Blazor** runs in two modes (covered below), **client-side Blazor** and **server-side Blazor**. Server-side Blazor does interact with the server on each web browser event; however, the entire web page <u>does not</u> need to be reloaded, so the speed on the application is usually just as fast as a **client-side Blazor** application.

Different Modes of Blazor

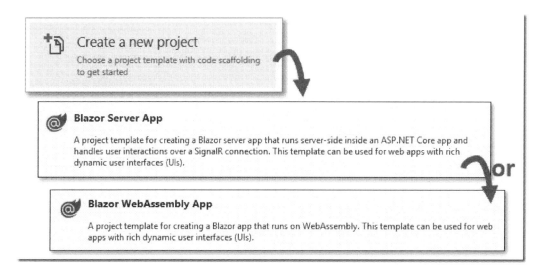

Blazor applications can be created in different modes. You can choose the mode when creating a new **Blazor** project in **Visual Studio**.

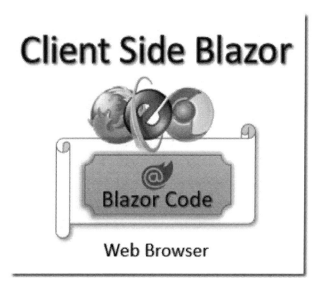

The **Blazor WebAssembly App** project template creates a **Blazor** project that runs in the user's web browser using **WebAssembly**, which is an open web standard and supported in all modern major web browsers.

The **Blazor** components are executed in this client-side runtime. This runtime communicates through a *JavaScript interop* that communicates with the web browser's **Document Object Model** (DOM) to update the web page and receive and process events and data.

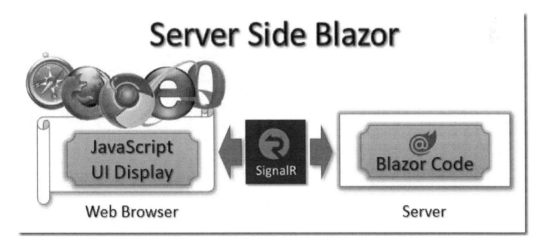

With **Blazor Server App**, the **Blazor** components are executed *server-side* and the runtime communicates with the web page using **SignalR,** which communicates with a **JavaScript interop** that communicates with the web browser's **Document Object Model** (DOM) to update the web page and receive and process events and data.

Blazor Features

Blazor contains a number of features that facilitate rapid construction of modern rich interactive applications.

Components

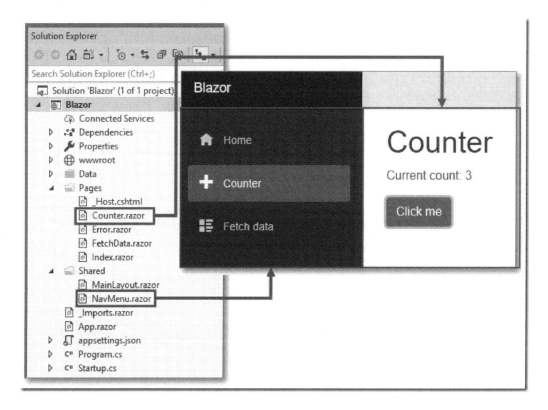

A **Blazor** application is composed of **Components**.

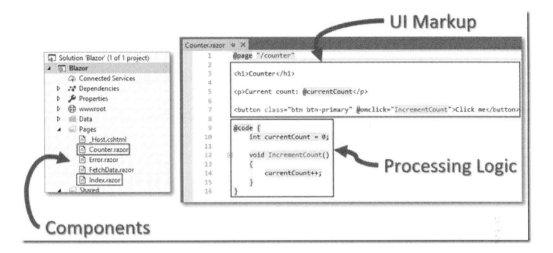

A **Component** is a *chunk* of code consisting of **User Interface (UI)** HTML markup **and** processing logic.

Data Binding

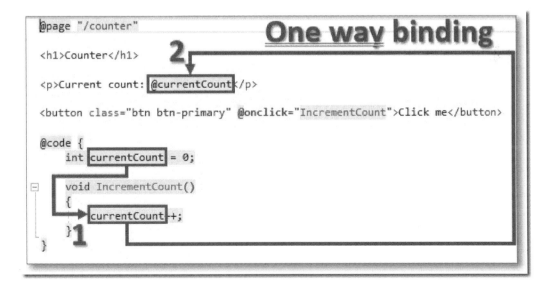

Blazor features **One-way** data binding…

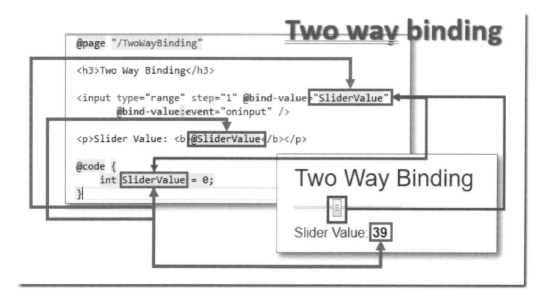

… and **Two-way** data binding.

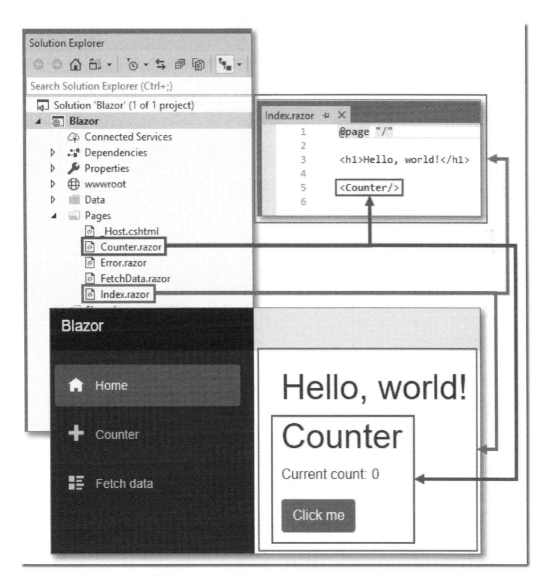

Components can be *nested inside* of other **Components**.

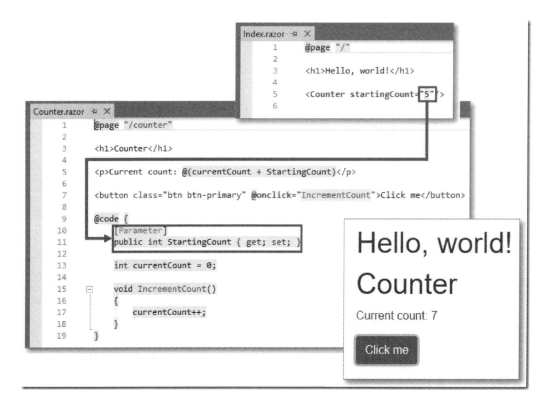

Components can *pass* parameters to other **Components**.

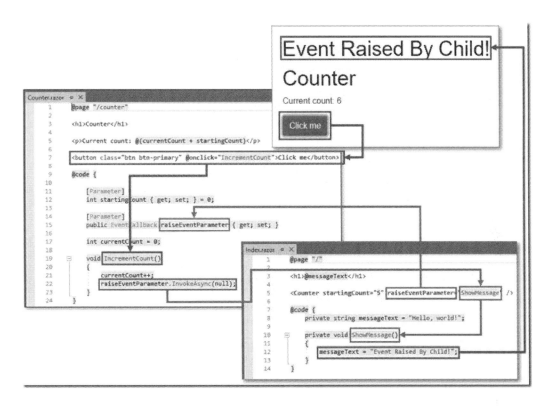

Components can *raise events* in other **Components**.

Routing

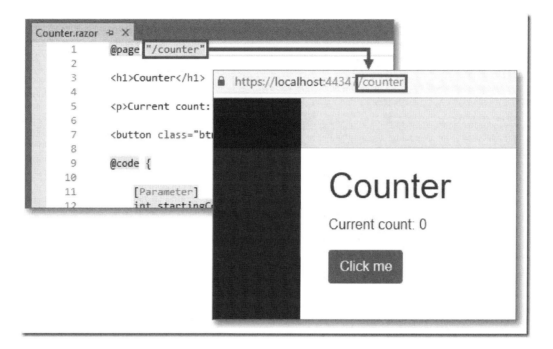

Routing in **Blazor** is as simple as using an **@page** directive and specifying a unique route for the control.

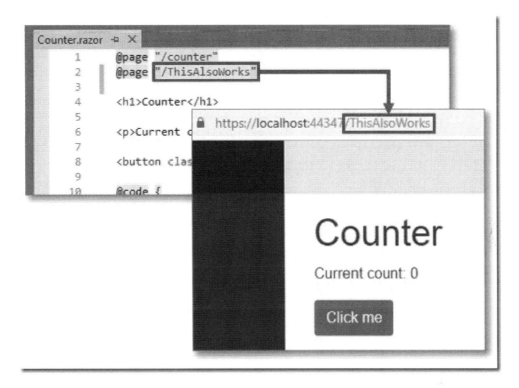

A control can even have multiple routes.

Forms and Validation

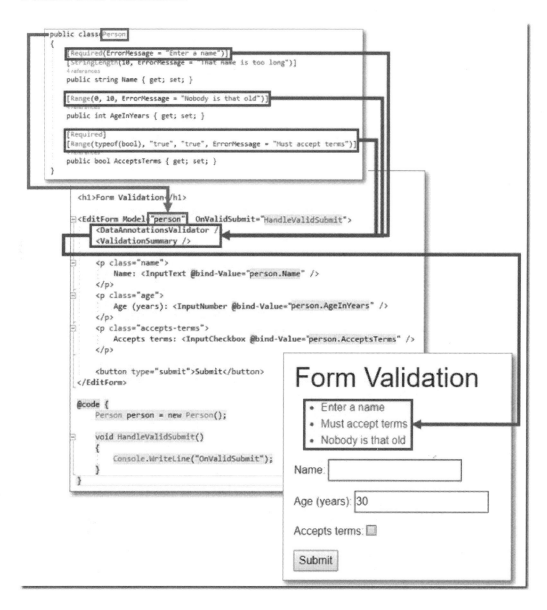

Blazor has additional features that one would require for a web application such as **Forms and Validation**.

For example, we can create a class, decorate it with *validation attributes*, and the validation will be implemented simply by using an **EditForm** control and a **DataAnnotationsValidator**, with a **ValidationsSummary** to display any errors.

JavaScript Interop

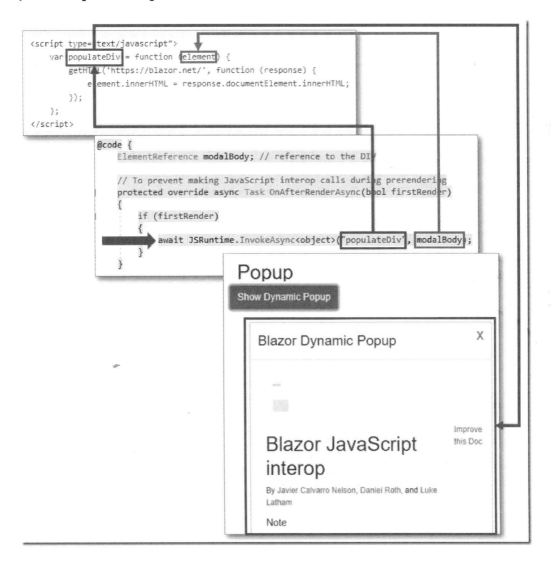

An Introduction to Building Applications with Blazor

With **Blazor**, you do not need to write any **JavaScript**. However, when you do need to interact with **JavaScript** (for example to make a call in the web browser to pull in page content from another site), you can use the built-in **JavaScript interop**.

Chapter 2: Getting Started

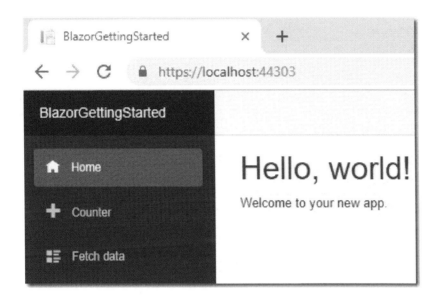

In this chapter, we will create a default **Blazor** project and explore the *components* and *features*.

To get started creating applications using **Microsoft Blazor**, the following are required:

Microsoft Windows 7 Service Pac 1 (or higher) or **Microsoft Windows Server 2012 R2 Service Pac 1** (or higher)

Visual Studio 2019 Version 16.3 (or higher) (Free download from: https://visualstudio.microsoft.com/free-developer-offers/)

.NET Core 3.0.0 SDK (or higher) (Free download from: https://dotnet.microsoft.com/download/dotnet-core/3.0)

Note: It is possible to develop **Blazor** applications using other methods. See this link for more information: https://docs.microsoft.com/en-us/aspnet/core/blazor/get-started.

Create the Default Project

Open **Visual Studio**.

Select **Create a new Project**.

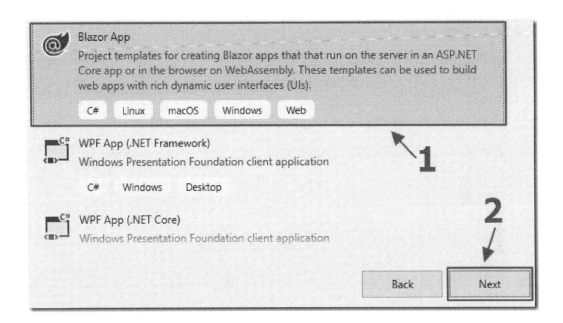

Select **Blazor App** and click **Next**.

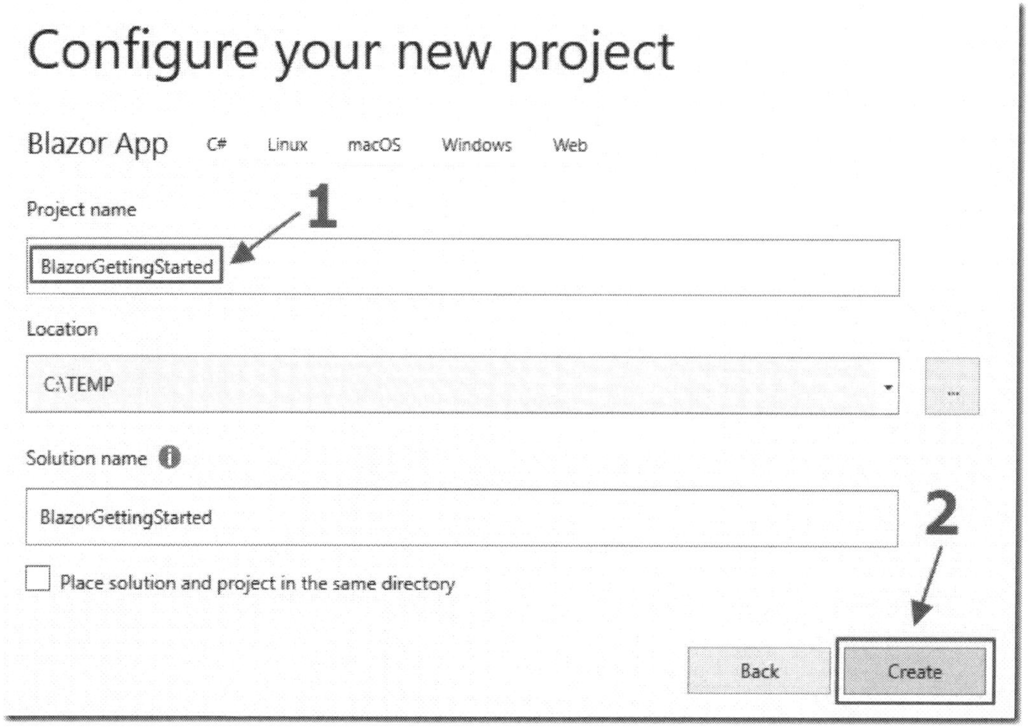

Configure your new project

Blazor App   C#   Linux   macOS   Windows   Web

Project name

1

| BlazorGettingStarted |

Location

| C:\TEMP | ▾ | ... |

Solution name ⓘ

| BlazorGettingStarted |

2

☐ Place solution and project in the same directory

| Back | | Create |

Give it a name and click **Create**.

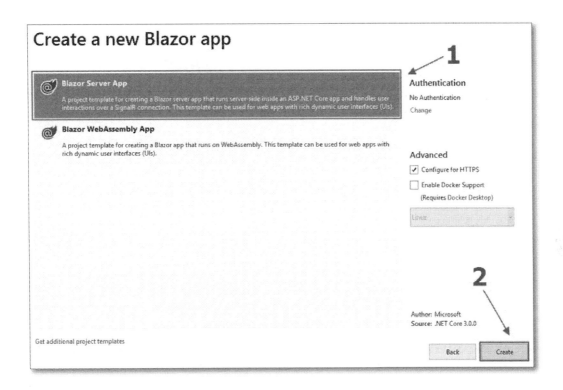

Select **Blazor Server App**.

Click **Create**.

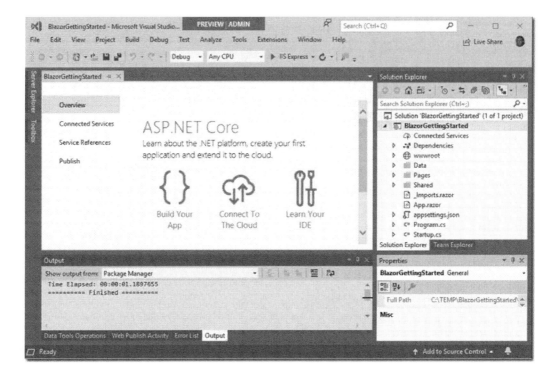

This will create the *default project*, and the application will open in **Visual Studio**.

Explore the Default Application

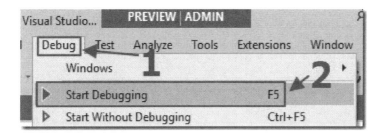

Select **Debug**, then **Start Debugging** to *run* the application.

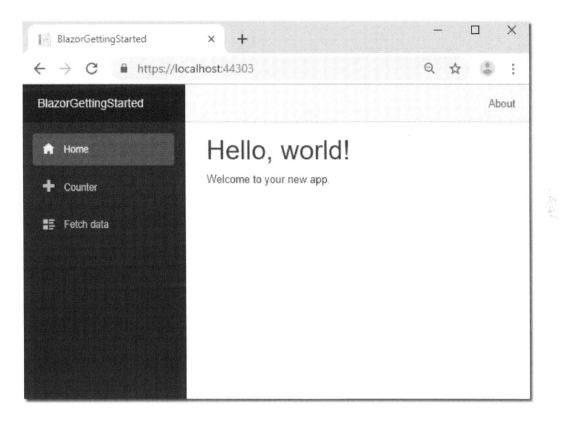

Your **web browser** will *open*, and the application will *load*.

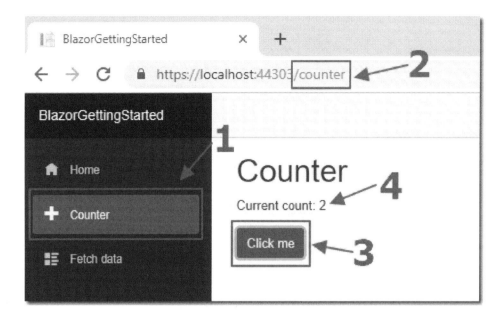

1. You can *click* on the **Counter** link to navigate to the **Counter** page
2. You will see that the url in your web browser changes to the */counter* address
3. You can *click* the **Click me** button
4. The number next to the **Current Count** label will *increase.*

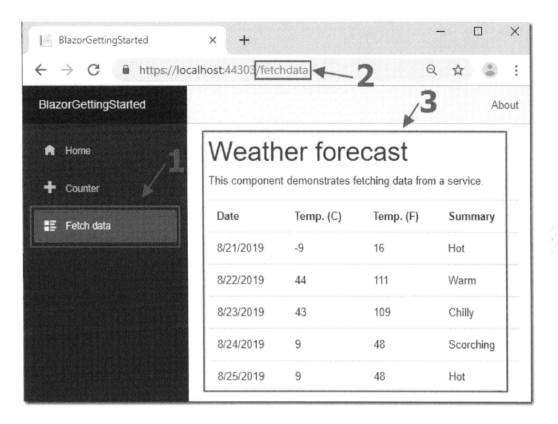

1. You can *click* on the **Fetch data** link to navigate to the **Weather forecast** page
2. You will see that the url in your web browser changes to the */fetchdata* address
3. A table of random weather forecasts will display.

An Introduction to Building Applications with Blazor

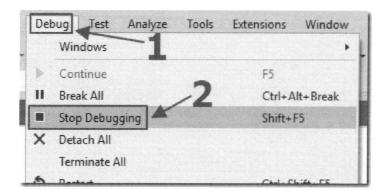

Return to **Visual Studio**, and select **Debug** then **Stop Debugging**.

Examine the Project Files

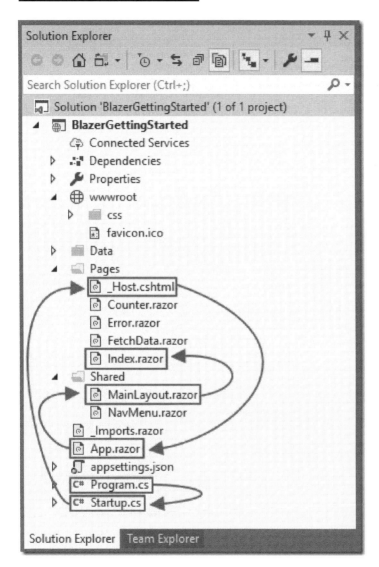

The **Solution Explorer** in **Visual Studio** allows us to see all the project files of the application.

The preceding diagram shows the order that the code is executed in (starting with the **Program.cs** file), to display the first page of the application (the default page of the application, that is contained in the **Index.razor** file).

The initial code that is loaded in the user's web browser is contained in the **_Host.cshtml** file. This creates a **HTML document** that loads the initial **.css** *style sheets* and *JavaScript files*, including the **Blazor.server.js** file that sets up the **SignalR** communication with the server.

This also loads the *application root* inside the **<app></app>** tags.

The code for the *application root* is contained in the **App.razor** control. This control sets up the *cascading parameters* used for security (covered in the chapter **Blazor Binding, Events and Parameters**) and the *routing*.

Routing and Layouts

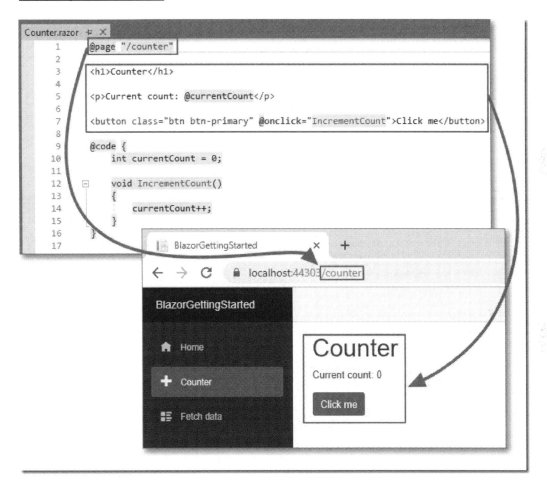

Every *routable* **Blazor** control must have a @page Razor directive with a unique *route*.

In this example, the **Counter** control, contained in the **Counter.razor** file, is configured by the @page directive to have the */counter* route.

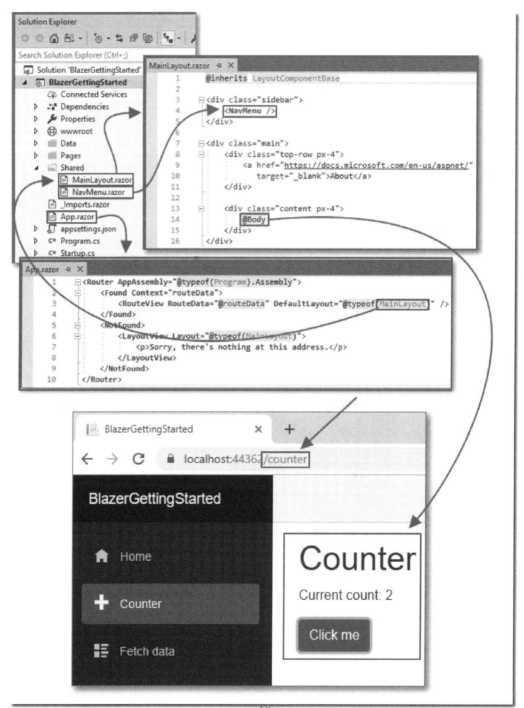

When the user navigates to the **/counter** route in their web browser, the **Counter** control is *loaded*, however, the **RouteView** in the **App.razor** file defines a *layout control* called **MainLayout**. This layout control will define the layout for that **RouteView**.

This **MainLayout** control is a *template* that defines the overall structure of the page that is returned.

It contains a @Body Razor directive that indicates where the content will go, in this case the **Counter** control.

The **MainLayout** control also loads other controls such as the **NavMenu** control (contained in the **NavMenu.razor** file), that contains the navigation menu that displays on the left-hand side of the resulting page.

Dependency Injection

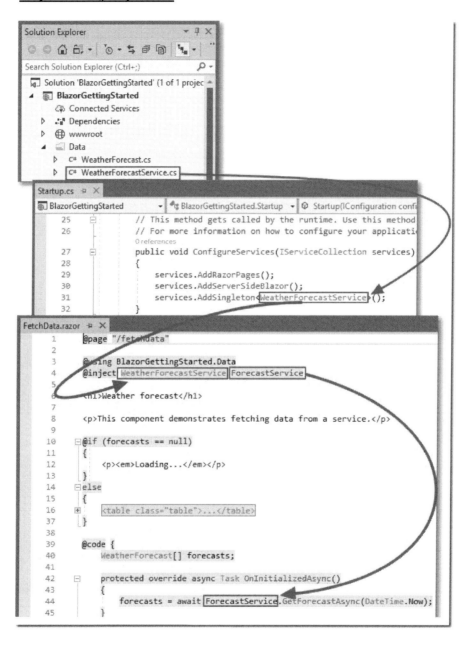

Services contained in **classes** can be *registered* in the **Startup.cs** file so that they are available to be *consumed* in **Blazor** components and classes using **Dependency Injection**.

For example, the **WeatherForecastService** class contained in the **WeatherForecastService.cs** code file is *registered* in the **ConfigureServices** section of the **Startup.cs** code file.

In this example, the service is registered as a **Singleton** (using **AddSingleton**—all requests use the same instance); however, in many cases, such as services that provide data for a single user, you will want to register your services as **Scoped** (using **AddScoped**—an instance of the service is created once per connection or client request).

```
FetchData.razor ↔ ×
 1      @page "/fetchdata"
 2
 3      @using BlazorGettingStarted.Data
 4      @inject WeatherForecastService ForecastService
 5
 6      <h1>Weather forecast</h1>
 7
 8      <p>This component demonstrates fetching data from a service.</p>
 9
10      @if (forecasts == null)...
14      @else...
38
39      @code {
40          WeatherForecast[] forecasts;
41
42          protected override async Task OnInitializedAsync()
43          {
44              forecasts = await ForecastService.GetForecastAsync(DateTime.Now)
45          }
```

```
WeatherForecastService.cs ↔ ×
BlazorGettingStarted              BlazorGettingStarted.Data.WeatherForecastS   Summaries
 1      using System;
 2      using System.Linq;
 3      using System.Threading.Tasks;
 4
 5      namespace BlazorGettingStarted.Data
 6      {
          5 references
 7          public class WeatherForecastService
 8          {
 9              private static readonly string[] Summaries = new[]...;
13
          2 references
14          public Task<WeatherForecast[]> GetForecastAsync(DateTime startDate)
15          {
16              var rng = new Random();
17              return Task.FromResult(Enumerable.Range(1, 5).Select(index => new WeatherForecast
18              {
19                  Date = startDate.AddDays(index),
20                  TemperatureC = rng.Next(-20, 55),
21                  Summary = Summaries[rng.Next(Summaries.Length)]
22              }).ToArray());
23          }
24      }
25  }
```

Also note that we are securely calling the **GetForecastAsync** method directly because we are using a *server-side* **Blazor** application.

Create a new Blazor app

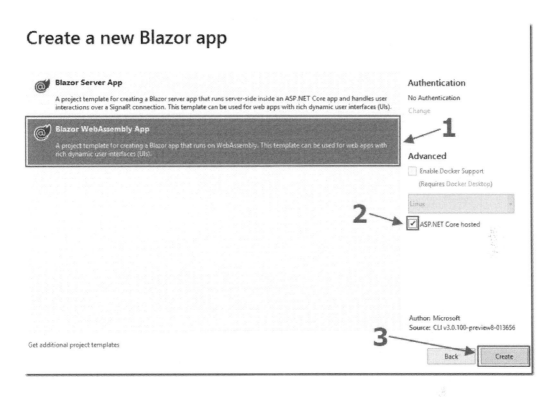

If, instead, we created a **Blazor WebAssembly App** that is **ASP.NET Core hosted**…

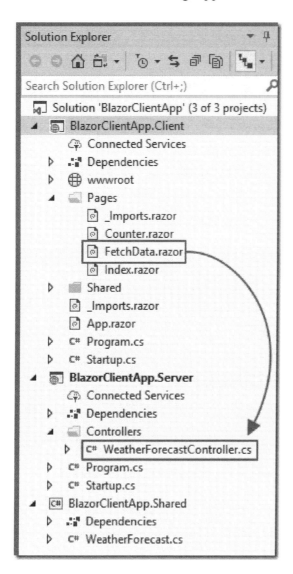

…we would have a different *project structure* that separates the code that runs in the *client web browser* (the **BlazorClientApp.Client** project) from the code that runs on the *server* (in the **BlazorClientApp.Server** project).

```
FetchData.razor  ⊕ X
   1     @page "/fetchdata"
   2     @using BlazorClientApp.Shared
   3     @inject HttpClient Http
   4
   5     <h1>Weather forecast</h1>
   6
   7     <p>This component demonstrates fetching data from the server.</p>
   8
   9  ⊞ @if (forecasts == null)...
  13  ⊞ else...
  37
  38     @code {
  39         WeatherForecast[] forecasts;
  40
  41  ⊟     protected override async Task OnInitializedAsync()
  42         {
  43             forecasts = await Http GetJsonAsync<WeatherForecast[]>("WeatherForecast");
  44         }
  45
  46     }
```

```
WeatherForecastController.cs  ⊕ X
🔲 BlazorClientApp.Server                    ▾  🔩 BlazorClientApp.Server.Controllers.WeatherForecastC▾
  26
  27             [HttpGet]
                 0 references | 0 requests | 0 exceptions
  28  ⊟         public IEnumerable<WeatherForecast> Get()     ◀━━  Http Call
  29             {
  30                 var rng = new Random();
  31  ⊟             return Enumerable.Range(1, 5).Select(index => new WeatherForecast
  32                 {
  33                     Date = DateTime.Now.AddDays(index),
  34                     TemperatureC = rng.Next(-20, 55),
  35                     Summary = Summaries[rng.Next(Summaries.Length)]
  36                 })
  37                 .ToArray();
  38             }
  39         }
  40     }
```

Because the *client* code is no longer running on the *server*, that version of the
FetchData.razor page has to make a *http request*, using the **GetJasonAsync**
method of the **HttpClient** (that was registered as a service in the **startup.cs** file),
to the method running on the *server*, which then returns the *weather forecast* data.

47

Chapter 3: Blazor Binding, Events and Parameters

The sample code for this chapter can be obtained at the link "Blazor Binding, Events and Parameters" at http://BlazorHelpWebsite.com/Downloads.aspx

The three things that you will usually find yourself using on every **Blazor** page, **Binding**, **Events**, and **Parameters**, will be covered here.

To demonstrate these, we will build a series of pages, including a few that will allow a user to build and edit a list of *To Do* items.

Create the Page

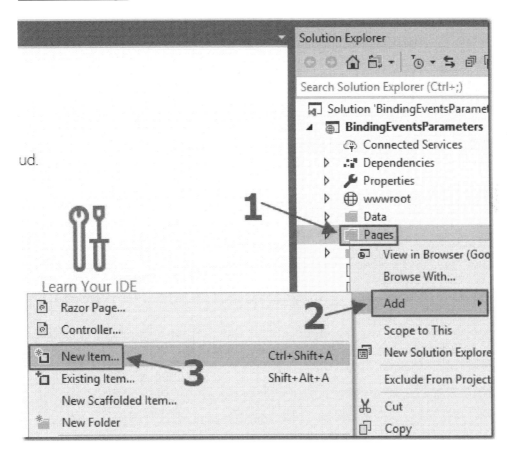

Create a new **server-side Blazor** project called **BindingEventsParameters**.

When the project opens in **Visual Studio,** *right-click* on the **Pages** folder and select **Add** then **New Item…**

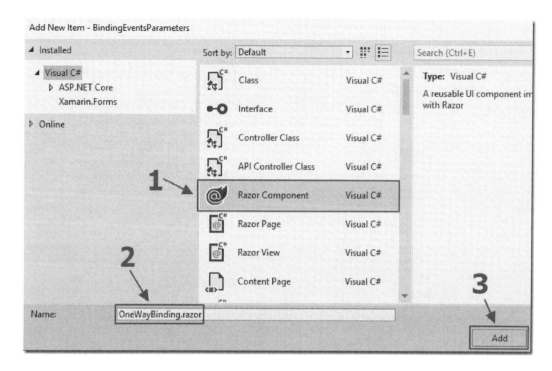

Select the **Razor Component** template, name the page **OneWayBinding.razor**, and click the **Add** button.

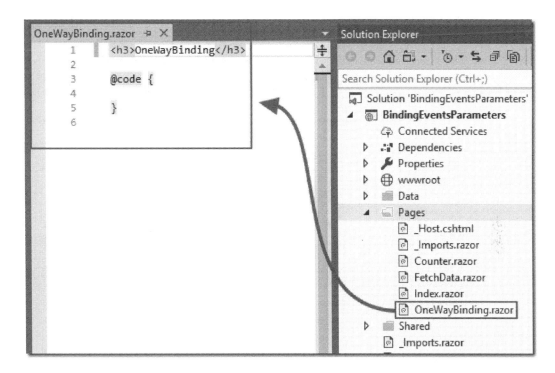

The page will display.

Add the following line to the top of the page to implement *routing* for the control:

```
@page "/OneWayBinding"
```

The final code should look like this:

```
@page "/OneWayBinding"
<h3>OneWayBinding</h3>
@code {
}
```

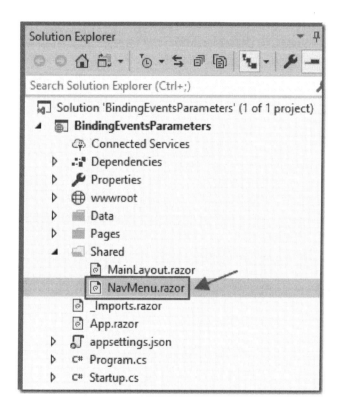

In the **Shared** folder, open the **NavMenu.razor** page.

Add the following to the menu control:

```
<li class="nav-item px-3">
    <NavLink class="nav-link" href="OneWayBinding">
        <span class="oi oi-list-rich" aria-hidden="true"></span> OneWay Binding
    </NavLink>
</li>
```

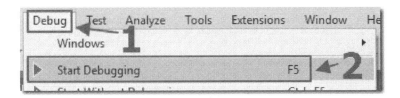

Hit **F5** to *run* the project…

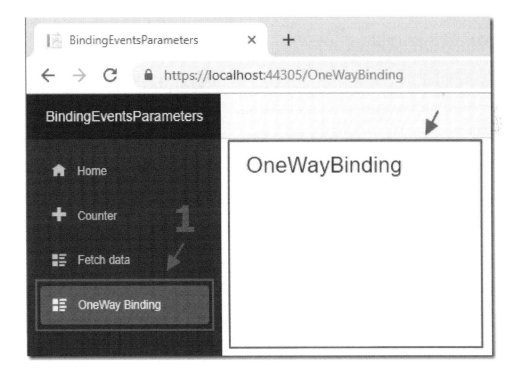

An Introduction to Building Applications with Blazor

When the application opens in the web browser, you can click the **OneWay Binding** link in the navigation, and the **OneWayBinding.razor** control will display.

In **Visual Studio**, select **Shift+F5** to stop the application.

One Way Binding

Binding allows you to **set** and **alter** a value in one part of your code and have it *display* in another part of your code.

For example, you can create a **property** in the **processing logic** of a control and display the *value* of that **property** in the **User Interface (UI) markup** of the control.

This is called *binding,* and it is achieved using the @bind attribute.

Alter the code of the **OneWayBinding.razor** control to the following:

```
@page "/OneWayBinding"
<h3>@Title</h3>
@code {
    string Title =
        "The name of this page is: One Way Binding";
}
```

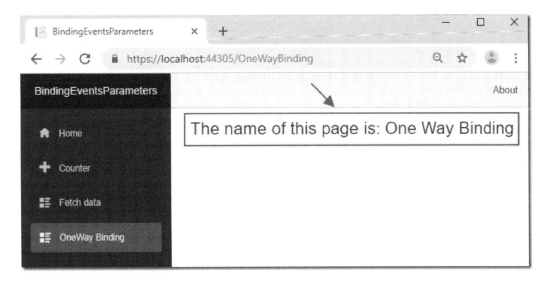

When we *run* the application, we see that the value we set for the *Title* variable displays in the **UI**.

```
OneWayBinding.razor  ⊡ ✕
1      @page "/OneWayBinding"
2      <h3>@Title</h3>
3
4      @code {
5          string Title =
6              "The name of this page is: One Way Binding";
7      }
8
```

Setting a value for a **variable** or a **property** and simply *consuming* it is called **one way binding**.

Two Way Binding

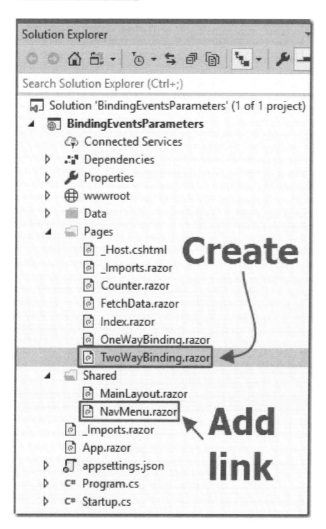

To demonstrate **two way** binding, create a new page called **TwoWayBinding.razor** and add a link to it in the **NavMenu.razor** control.

Use the following code for the **TwoWayBinding.razor** control:

```
@page "/TwoWayBinding"
<h3>Two Way Binding</h3>
<p>Slider Value: <b>@SliderValue</b></p>
@code {
    int SliderValue = 0;
}
```

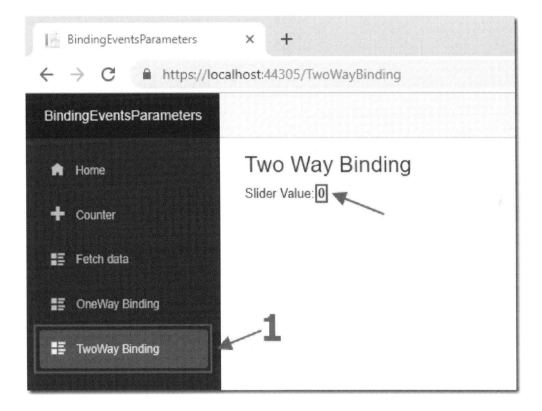

When we *run* the project and *navigate* to the control, we see the **SliderValue** is set to *zero* using **one way binding**.

Stop the project and *add* the following code to the **UI markup**:

```
<input type="range" step="1"
       @bind-value="SliderValue"
       @bind-value:event="oninput" />
```

This adds a **slider** control to the page that is bound to the **SliderValue** variable. However, this time we are using the @bind-value attribute. Using this allows us to specify an *event parameter* for the @bind-value attribute.

In this case, we have selected the *oninput* parameter that will update the **SliderValue** variable with the current **slider** value each time the **slider** value changes.

If we did not use the *oninput* parameter, the **SliderValue** variable would not update until we clicked away from the **slider** control.

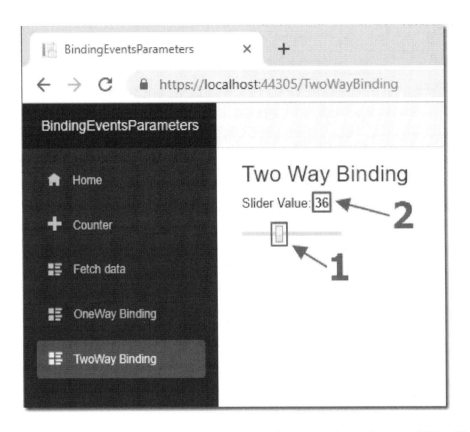

When we *run* the project, we can move the **slider** bound to the **SliderValue** variable, and the **SliderValue** variable is updated immediately and *displayed*.

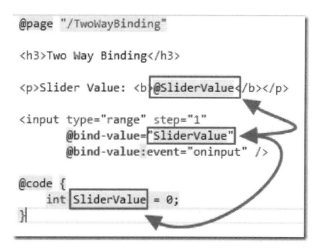

When we *manipulate* a variable or property through a **UI control**, rather than just *consuming* it, we are implementing **two way binding**, because the *consumer* is updating the *source*.

Create a To Do Page

Let's take what we learned so far about *binding* and create the classic *To Do* application.

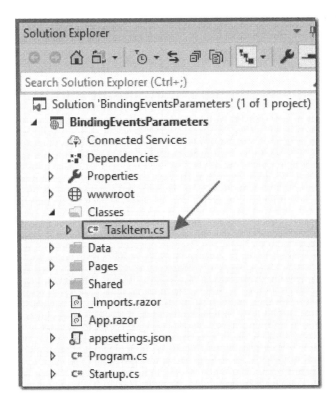

Create a new *folder* called **Classes** and add a **class** called **TaskItem.cs** using the following code:

```csharp
using System;
namespace BindingEventsParameters
{
    public class TaskItem
    {
        public string TaskDescription { get; set; }
        public bool IsComplete { get; set; }
    }
}
```

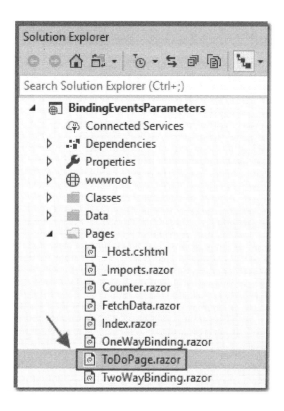

Next, add a new page called **ToDoPage.razor** to the **Pages** folder (also add a link to the control in the **NavMenu.razor** page).

Change *all* the code in the **ToDoPage.razor** control to the following:

```
@page "/ToDoPage"
<h3>ToDo Page</h3>
<br />
<ul class="list-group">
    @foreach (var Task in Tasks)
    {
        <!-- Use @key to ensure correct Blazor -->
        <!-- diffing algorithm behavior when binding a list -->
        <li @key="Task"
            class="list-group-item form-check form-check-inline">
            <input type="checkbox"
                   class="form-check-input"
                   @bind-value="Task.IsComplete" />
            <label class="form-check-label"
                   for="inlineCheckbox1">
                @Task.TaskDescription
            </label>
        </li>
    }
</ul>
@code {
    // Collection to hold all the Tasks
    private List<TaskItem> Tasks = new List<TaskItem>();
    // This method will run when the control is loaded
    protected override void OnInitialized()
    {
        // Add a Task
        Tasks.Add(new TaskItem()
        {
            TaskDescription = "Task One",
            IsComplete = false
        });
    }
}
```

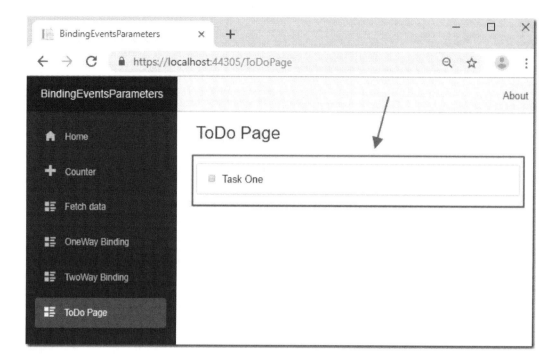

When we *run* the application, we see that a **Task** will be displayed using **one way binding**.

Now, to implement the functionality to add a **Task**, add the following **UI markup**:

```
<br />
<div class="container">
    <div class="row">
        <div class="col">
            <input class="form-control"
                    placeholder="Add a Task"
                    @bind-value="newTaskDescription" />
        </div>
        <div class="col">
            <button class="btn btn-primary"
                    type="button"
                    @onclick="AddTask">
                Add Task
            </button>
        </div>
    </div>
</div>
```

Add the following code to implement the **AddTask** method:

```
// Property to hold the description of a new Task
// The textbox is bound to this property
private string newTaskDescription;
private void AddTask()
{
    if (!string.IsNullOrWhiteSpace(newTaskDescription))
    {
        // Create a new Task
        // using the current value of the
        // newTaskDescription property
        var NewTask = new TaskItem();
        NewTask.TaskDescription = newTaskDescription;
        NewTask.IsComplete = false;
        // Add the new Task to the collection
        Tasks.Add(NewTask);
        // Clear the newTaskDescription value
        // so the text box will now be empty
        newTaskDescription = string.Empty;
    }
}
```

When we run the application, we can enter a new **Task** and click the **Add Task** button.

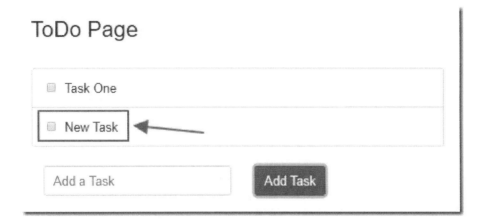

The **Task** is then *added* to the **Tasks collection**, and automatically displayed in the list.

The following diagram shows how the *binding* works:

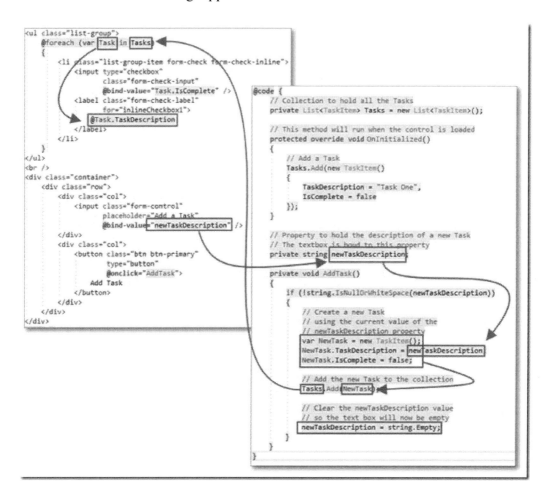

We can also add a **Delete** button to the list, which will *pass* the current **Task** to the **RemoveTask** method, in the *onclick* event:

```
<button type="button" class="btn btn-link"
        @onclick="(() => RemoveTask(Task))">
    [Delete]
</button>
```

We then add code to implement the **RemoveTask** method:

```
private void RemoveTask(TaskItem paramTaskItem)
{
    // Remove the Task from the collection
    Tasks.Remove(paramTaskItem);
}
```

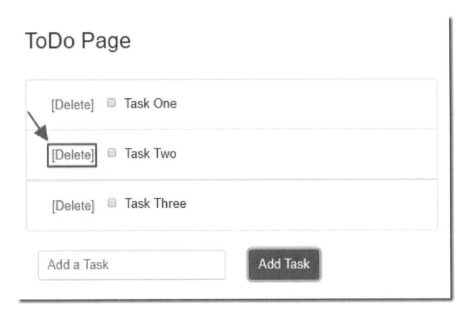

When we *run* the application, we can *click* the **[Delete]** button next to a **Task**…

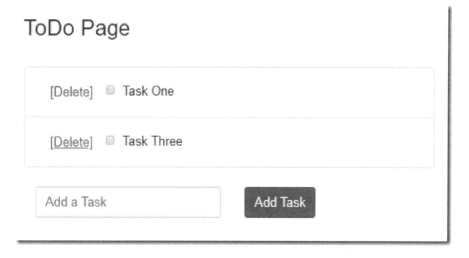

…and the **Task** will be removed for the *collection*, and the list will be automatically *updated*.

Finally, we can add the following **UI markup** to the page:

```
<p>
    Tasks: <b>@(Tasks.Count())</b>
    Completed:
    <b>@(Tasks.Where(x => x.IsComplete == true).Count())</b>
</p>
```

This will automatically display a *count* of the **Tasks**, and track the number of **Tasks** marked *completed*.

```
<p>
    Tasks: <b>@(Tasks.Count())</b>
    Completed:
    <b>@Tasks.Where(x => x.IsComplete == true).Count())</b>
</p>
<ul class="list-group">
    @foreach (var Task in Tasks)
    {
    <li class="list-group-item form-check form-check-inline">
        <button type="button" class="btn btn-link"
            @onclick="(() => RemoveTask(Task))">
        [Delete]
        </button>
        <input type="checkbox"
            class="form-check-input"
            @bind-value="Task.IsComplete" />
        <label class="form-check-label"
            for="inlineCheckbox1">
        @Task.TaskDescription
        </label>
    </li>
    }
</ul>
```

This demonstrates how *bindings* to **properties** are automatically updated in the **UI** whenever **Blazor** detects there are *changes* to the *values*.

Parameters

Parameters allow one **control** to set the value of **properties** on another **control**.

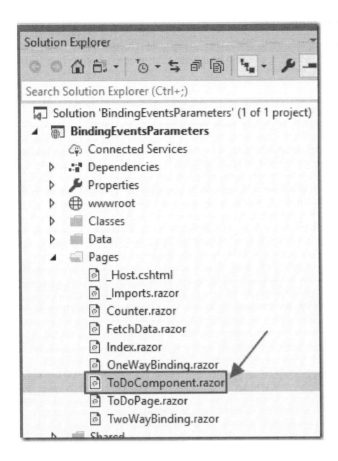

Create a new page called **ToDoComponent.razor** using the following code:

```
<ul class="list-group">
    @foreach (var Task in Tasks)
    {
        <li class="list-group-item form-check form-check-inline">
            <label class="form-check-label"
                for="inlineCheckbox1">
                @Task.TaskDescription
            </label>
        </li>
    }
</ul>
@code {
    // Collection to hold the Tasks
    // passed in by the parent component
    [Parameter] public List<TaskItem> Tasks { get; set; }
}
```

Note that we did not define a @page attribute because we do not need *routing* to this component. This component will be directly consumed by a *parent component*.

Change the **UI markup** of the **ToDo.razor** page to the following:

```
@page "/ToDoPage"
<h3>ToDo Page</h3>
<br />
<ToDoComponent Tasks="Tasks" />
```

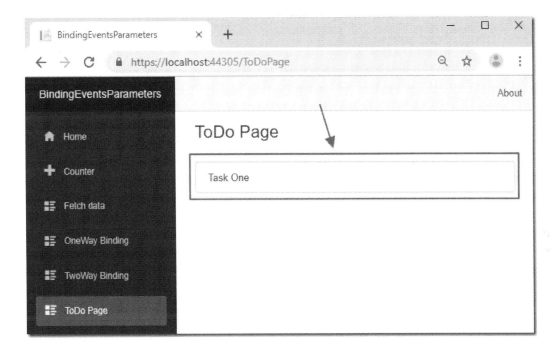

When we run the application, we see that the **Tasks collection** from the *parent* component (**ToDo.razor**) is passed as a *parameter* and displayed in the list in the *child* component (**ToDoComponent.razor**).

```
ToDoPage.razor  ⚲  ✕
    1       @page "/ToDoPage"
    2       <h3>ToDo Page</h3>
    3       <br />
    4       <ToDoComponent Tasks="Tasks" />
    5       @code {
    6           // Collection to hold all the Tasks
    7           private List<TaskItem> Tasks = new List<TaskItem>();
    8
    9           // This method will run when the control is loaded
   10           protected override void OnInitialized()
   11           {
   12               // Add a Task
   13               Tasks.Add(new TaskItem()
   14               {
   15                   TaskDescription = "Task One",
   16                   IsComplete = false
   17               });
   18           }
   19
```

```
ToDoComponent.razor  ⚲  ✕
    1       <ul class="list-group">
    2           @foreach (var Task in Tasks)
    3           {
    4               <li class="list-group-item form-check form-check-inline">
    5                   <label class="form-check-label"
    6                       for="inlineCheckbox1">
    7                       @Task.TaskDescription
    8                   </label>
    9               </li>
   10           }
   11       </ul>
   12       @code {
   13
   14           // Collection to hold the Tasks
   15           // passed in by the parent component
   16           [Parameter] public List<TaskItem> Tasks { get; set; }
   17       }
```

This is essentially *binding* as we explored earlier; however, it is **one way binding**.

Calling a Method on a Child Component

While **parameters** allows us to *pass values* from a *parent* control to a *child* control, it will not allow us to *invoke* a method on a *child* control.

One method that will allow this is the @ref attribute.

Add the following code to the **ToDoComponent.razor** page:

```
// This method will be called directly by the parent
// component
public void AddNewTask(TaskItem paramTaskItem)
{
    // Add the new Task to the collection
    Tasks.Add(paramTaskItem);
}
```

Add the following *property* to the **ToDoPage.razor** control:

```
// This will hold a reference to the ToDoComponent
private ToDoComponent ToDoComponentControl;
```

Change the **AddTask** method to the following:

```csharp
private void AddTask()
{
    if (!string.IsNullOrWhiteSpace(newTaskDescription))
    {
        // Create a new Task
        // using the current value of the
        // newTaskDescription property
        var NewTask = new TaskItem();
        NewTask.TaskDescription = newTaskDescription;
        NewTask.IsComplete = false;
        // Add the new Task to the collection
        // by calling a method on the child component
        ToDoComponentControl.AddNewTask(NewTask);
        // Clear the newTaskDescription value
        // so the text box will now be empty
        newTaskDescription = string.Empty;
    }
}
```

Next, implement the @ref attribute on the **ToDoComponent** in the **UI markup**, so it now reads:

```
<ToDoComponent Tasks="Tasks"
               @ref="ToDoComponentControl" />
```

Finally, add an **input control** and a **button** to add new **Tasks**:

```
<br />
<div class="container">
    <div class="row">
        <div class="col">
            <input class="form-control"
                   placeholder="Add a Task"
                   @bind-value="newTaskDescription" />
        </div>
        <div class="col">
            <button class="btn btn-primary"
                    type="button"
                    @onclick="AddTask">
                Add Task
            </button>
        </div>
    </div>
</div>
```

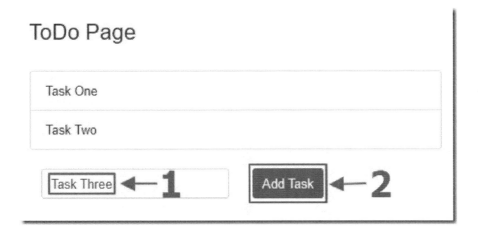

When we run the application, we are able to add **Tasks** from the *parent* control by calling the method on the *child* control.

```
18        <ToDoComponent Tasks="Tasks"
20                       @ref="ToDoComponentControl" />
21    <br />
22    <div class="container">
23        <div class="row">
24            <div class="col">
25                <input class="form-control"
26                       placeholder="Add a Task"
27                       @bind-value="newTaskDescription" />
28            </div>
29            <div class="col">
30                <button class="btn btn-primary"
31                        type="button"
32                        @onclick="AddTask">
33                    Add Task
34                </button>
35            </div>
36        </div>
37    </div>
38    @code {
39        ToDoComponent ToDoComponentControl;
40
41        private void AddTask()
42        {
43            if (!string.IsNullOrWhiteSpace(newTaskDescription))
44            {
45                // Create a new Task
46                // using the current value of the
47                // newTaskDescription property
48                var NewTask = new TaskItem();
49                NewTask.TaskDescription = newTaskDescription;
50                NewTask.IsComplete = false;
51
52                // Add the new Task to the collection
53                // by calling a method on the child component
54                ToDoComponentControl.AddNewTask(NewTask);
55
56                // Clear the newTaskDescription value
57                // so the text box will now be empty
58                newTaskDescription = string.Empty;
59            }
60
```

```
ToDoComponent.razor
3        {
4            <li class="list-group-item form-check form-check-inline">
5                <button type="button" class="btn btn-link"
6                        @onclick="(() => RemoveTask(Task))">
7                    [Delete]
8                </button>
9                <label class="form-check-label"
10                       for="inlineCheckbox1">
11                    @Task.TaskDescription
12                </label>
13            </li>
14        }
15    </ul>
16    @code {
17        // Collection to hold the Tasks
18        // passed in by the parent component
19        [Parameter] public List<TaskItem> Tasks { get; set; }
20
21        // This method will be called directly by the parent
22        // component
23        public void AddNewTask(TaskItem paramTaskItem)
24        {
25            // Add the new Task to the collection
26            Tasks.Add(paramTaskItem);
27        }
28    }
```

The diagram above illustrates how a *reference* is made on the **ToDoComponent** control, using the @ref attribute, and how that reference is then used to call the **AddNewTask** method on that control.

Events

We have explored various methods to communicate from a *parent* component to a *child* component. *Events*, using **EventCallback**, provides a method that allows a **child component** to communicate with a **parent component**.

Add the following code to **ToDoComponent.razor**:

```
// RemoveTaskChanged is an EventCallback that will
// notify the parent component when an item is to be removed
// passing the item to be removed
[Parameter] public EventCallback<TaskItem> RemoveTaskChanged { get; set; }
private async Task RemoveTask(TaskItem paramTaskItem)
{
    // Notify parent component to
    // Remove the Task from the collection
    await RemoveTaskChanged.InvokeAsync(paramTaskItem);
}
```

Also, add a **delete button** (that will appear next to each list item), which will call the **RemoveTask** method (also passing the current **Task**):

```
<button type="button" class="btn btn-link"
        @onclick="(() => RemoveTask(Task))">
    [Delete]
</button>
```

When we look at **ToDoPage.razor** we see we already have this method to *remove* a **Task** from the *collection*:

```
private void RemoveTask(TaskItem paramTaskItem)
{
    // Remove the Task from the collection
    Tasks.Remove(paramTaskItem);
}
```

Finally, we need to update the **ToDoComponent** tag to indicate that the **RemoveTask** method is to be *invoked* when the **RemovedTaskChanged** ev*ent handler* is invoked in the *child control* (**ToDoComponent.razor**):

```
<ToDoComponent Tasks="Tasks"
               @ref="ToDoComponentControl"
               RemoveTaskChanged="RemoveTask" />
```

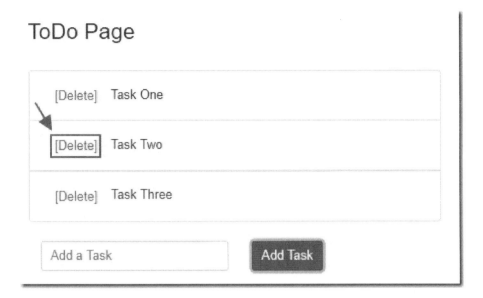

When we run the application, we can now click the **[Delete]** button...

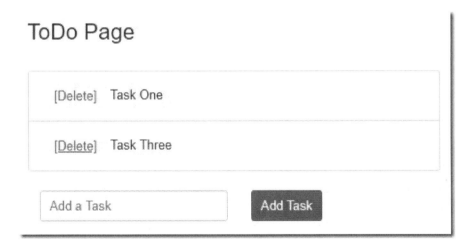

... to remove a **Task** from the list.

```
ToDoPage.razor
    4        <ToDoComponent Tasks="Tasks"
    5                    @ref="ToDoComponentControl"
    6              RemoveTaskChanged="RemoveTask" />
    7
    8        <br />
    9        <div class="container">
   10            <div class="row">
   11                <div class="col">
   12                    <input class="form-control"
   13                           placeholder="Add a Task"
   14                           @bind-value="newTaskDescription" />
   15                </div>
   16                <div class="col">
   17                    <button class="btn btn-primary"
   18                            type="button"
   19                            @onclick="AddTask">
   20                        Add Task
   21                    </button>
   22                </div>
   23            </div>
   24        </div>
   25        @code {
   26            // This will hold a reference to the ToDoComponent
   27            private ToDoComponent ToDoComponentControl;
   28
   29            private void RemoveTask(TaskItem paramTaskItem)
   30            {
   31                // Remove the Task from the collection
   32                Tasks.Remove(paramTaskItem);
   33            }
```

```
ToDoComponent.razor
    1        <ul class="list-group">
    2            @foreach (var Task in Tasks)
    3            {
    4                <li class="list-group-item form-check form-check-inline">
    5                    <button type="button" class="btn btn-link"
    6                            @onclick="(() => RemoveTask(Task))">
    7                        [Delete]
    8                    </button>
    9                    <label class="form-check-label"
   10                           for="inlineCheckbox1">
   11                        @Task.TaskDescription
   12                    </label>
   13                </li>
   14            }
   15        </ul>
   16        @code {
   17            // Collection to hold the Tasks
   18            // passed in by the parent component
   19            [Parameter] public List<TaskItem> Tasks { get; set; }
   20
   21            // RemoveTaskChanged is an EventCallback that will
   22            // notify the parent component when an item is to be removed
   23            // passing the item to be removed
   24            [Parameter] public EventCallback<TaskItem> RemoveTaskChanged { get; set; }
   25            private async RemoveTask(TaskItem paramTaskItem)
   26            {
   27                // Notify parent component to
   28                // Remove the Task from the collection
   29                await RemoveTaskChanged.InvokeAsync(paramTaskItem)
   30            }
```

The diagram above shows how the **child component** raises the **event** by calling **InvokeAsync**, passing the currently selected **Task** as a **parameter**.

Cascading Parameters

The final example will demonstrate *cascading parameters*. A **cascading parameter** is different from a normal **parameter** in that the *value* of the **cascading parameter** will pass to *all* child controls, no matter how deeply *nested*, that declare the parameter.

Add the following code to **ToDoPage.razor**:

```
// SelectedColor will be the cascading parameter
// Set the color to Green
protected string SelectedColor { get; set; } = "Green";
// Create a collection of colors that will be bound to a dropdown
List<string> Options = new List<string>() { "Green", "Red", "Blue" };
```

Add the following **UI markup** to the page, to display the currently **selected color** and a **dropdown** to allow it to be changed:

```
<label for="Summary">Theme Color: </label>
<select class="form-control"
        @bind="@SelectedColor">
    @foreach (var option in Options)
    {
        <option value="@option">
            @option
        </option>
    }
</select>
<br />
```

Finally, surround the **ToDoComponent** tag with the **CascadingValue** tag. *Name* the *cascading parameter* **ThemeColor**, and pass the **SelectedColor** variable as its *Value*:

```
<CascadingValue Value=SelectedColor Name="ThemeColor">
    <ToDoComponent Tasks="Tasks"
                   @ref="ToDoComponentControl"
                   RemoveTaskChanged="RemoveTask" />
</CascadingValue>
```

In **ToDoComponent.razor** add the following code:

```
// Declare the ThemeColor CascadingParameter
// from the ancestor control as ThemeColorParameter
[CascadingParameter(Name = "ThemeColor")]
protected string ThemeColorParameter { get; set; }
```

Next, alter the label in the **UI markup** to the following, to allow the **color** to be set by the value of **ThemeColorParameter**:

```
<label class="form-check-label"
       for="inlineCheckbox1"
       style="color:@ThemeColorParameter">
```

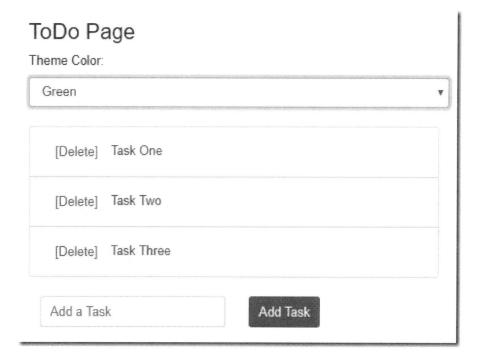

We can run the application…

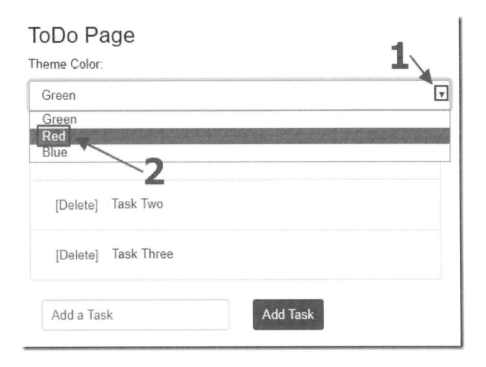

… *change* the value of the **cascading parameter**…

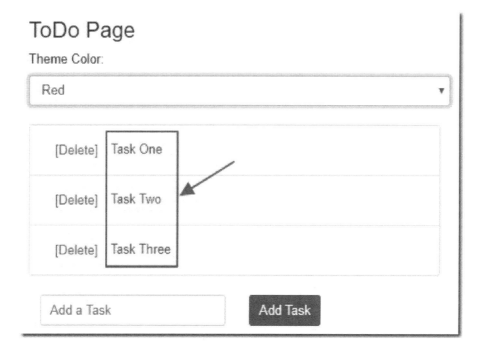

… and the **value** is immediately *updated* on *all* **child components** that declare and implement the parameter.

```
ToDoPage.razor ⊣ ✕
 1      @page "/ToDoPage"
 2      <h3>ToDo Page</h3>
 3      <label for="Summary">Theme Color: </label>
 4    ⊟<select class="form-control"
 5              @bind="@SelectedColor">
 6    ⊟    @foreach (var option in Options)
 7          {
 8    ⊟        <option value="@option">
 9                  @option
10              </option>
11          }
12      </select>
13      <br />
14    ⊟<CascadingValue Value=SelectedColor  Name="ThemeColor">
15          <ToDoComponent Tasks="Tasks"
16                         @ref="ToDoComponentControl"
17                         RemoveTaskChanged="RemoveTask" />
18      </CascadingValue>
19      <br />
20    ⊞<div class="container">...</div>
36      @code {
37    ⊟    // SelectedColor will be the cascading parameter
38          // Set the color to Green
39          protected string SelectedColor { get; set; } = "Green";
40
41          // Create a collection of colors that will be bound to a dropdown
42          List<string> Options = new List<string>() { "Green", "Red", "Blue" };
43
```

```
ToDoComponent.razor ⊣ ✕
 1    ⊟<ul class="list-group">
 2    ⊟    @foreach (var Task in Tasks)
 3          {
 4    ⊟        <li class="list-group-item form-check form-check-inline">
 5    ⊟            <button type="button" class="btn btn-link"
 6                         @onclick="(() => RemoveTask(Task))">
 7                      [Delete]
 8                  </button>
 9    ⊟            <label class="form-check-label"
10                         for="inlineCheckbox1"
11                         style="color:@ThemeColorParameter">
12                      @Task.TaskDescription
13                  </label>
14              </li>
15          }
16      </ul>
17      @code {
18    ⊟        // Declare the ThemeColor CascadingParameter
19              // from the ancestor control as ThemeColorParameter
20              [CascadingParameter(Name = "ThemeColor")]
21              protected string ThemeColorParameter { get; set; }
22
```

91

An Introduction to Building Applications with Blazor

The diagram above shows how the **cascading parameter** is *declared* and *consumed*.

Chapter 4: Creating a Step-By-Step End-To-End Database Server-Side Blazor Application

The sample code for this chapter can be obtained at the link "Creating A Step-By-Step End-To-End Database Server-Side Blazor Application" at http://BlazorHelpWebsite.com/Downloads.aspx

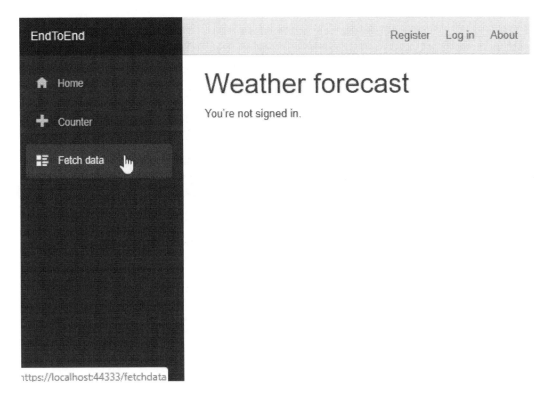

The primary benefit we have when using **server-side Blazor** is that we do not have to make *web http* calls from the client code to the server code. This reduces the code we need to write and eliminates many security concerns.

93

In this chapter, we will demonstrate how a list of **Weather forecasts** can be added to the database by each user. A user will only have the ability to see their own forecasts.

Use SQL Server

The new project template in **Visual Studio** will allow you to create a database using **SQL Server Express LocalDB**. However, it can be problematic to install and configure. Using the free **SQL Server 2017 Developer server** (or the full **SQL Server**) is recommended.

Download and install **SQL Server 2017 Developer Edition** from the following link:

https://www.microsoft.com/en-us/sql-server/sql-server-downloads

Create the Blazor Application

Open **Visual Studio**.

Select **Create a new Project**.

An Introduction to Building Applications with Blazor

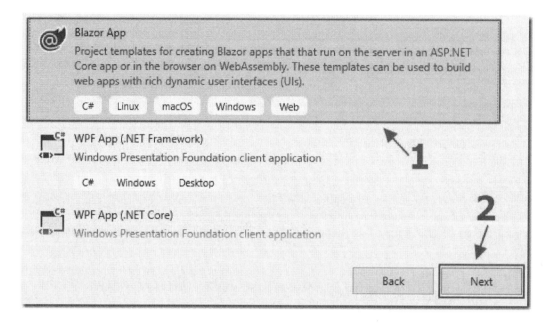

Select **Blazor App** and click **Next**.

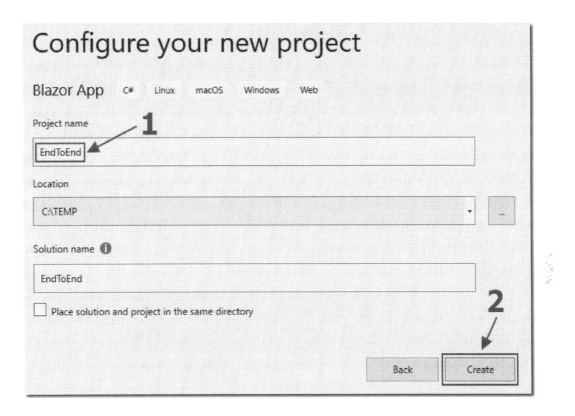

Give it a name and click **Create**.

Select **Blazor Server App**.

Click the **Change** link under **Authentication**.

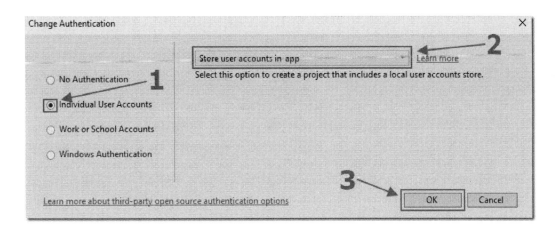

Select **Individual User Accounts** and **Store user accounts in-app**.

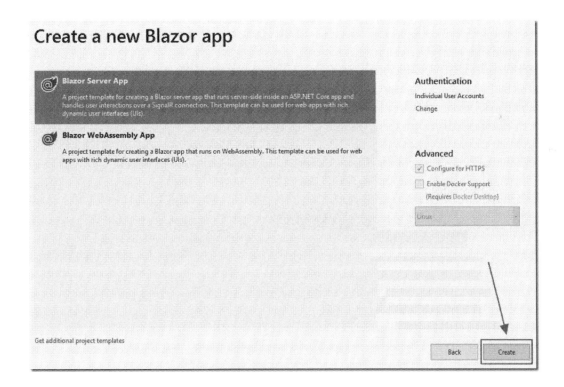

Click **Create**.

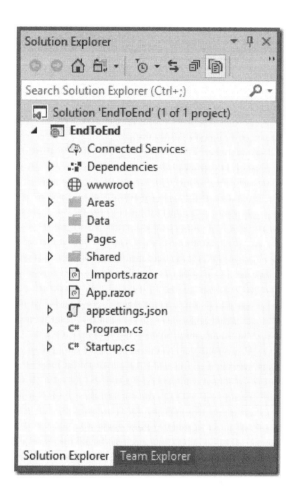

The **project** will be created.

Create the Database

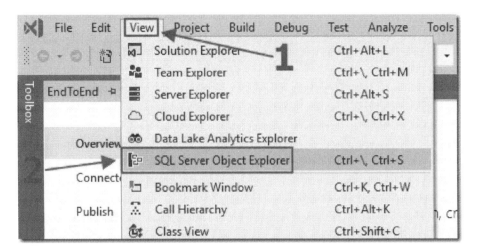

Open the **SQL Server Object Explorer**.

Add a connection to your **local database server** if you don't already have it in the **SQL Server** list.

For this tutorial, we do not want to use the **SQL Express server** on **(localdb)** that you may already see in the list.

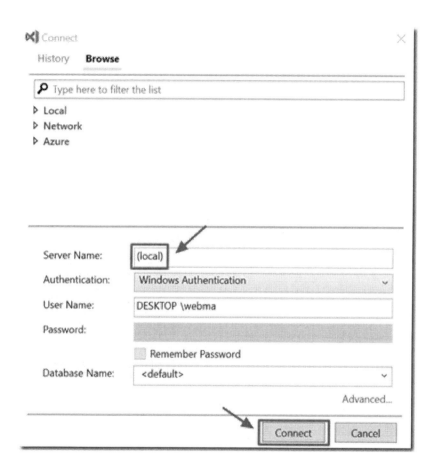

You will specify just the server and **Connect**.

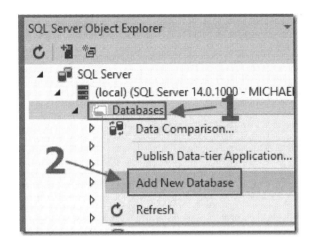

Expand the tree under the local **SQL server**, *right-click* on the **Databases** folder and select **Add New Database**.

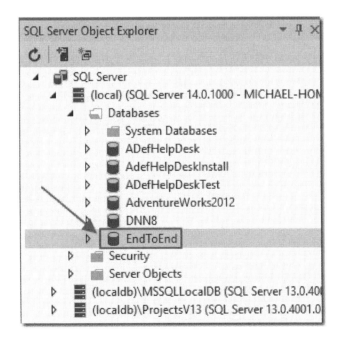

Give the **database** a name and press **Enter**.

The **database** will be created.

Click on the **Database** node.

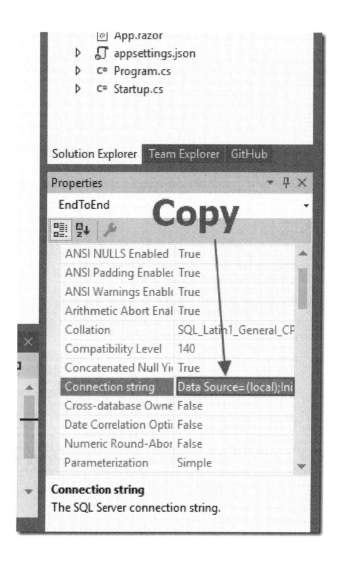

Open the **Properties** window if it is not already opened.

The **properties** for the **database** will display.

Copy the **Connection string** for the **database**.

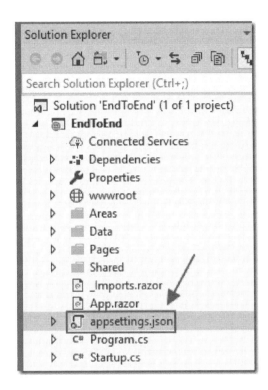

Open the **appsettings.json** file.

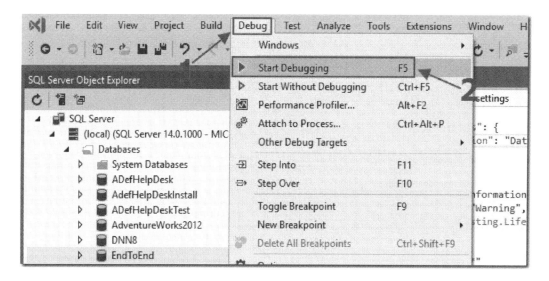

Paste in the **connection string** for the **DefaultConnection** and **save** the file.

Hit **F5** to run the application.

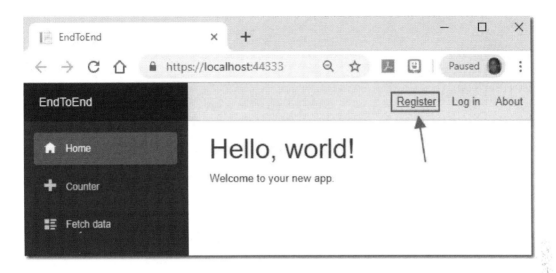

The application will open in your **web browser**.

Click the **Register** link.

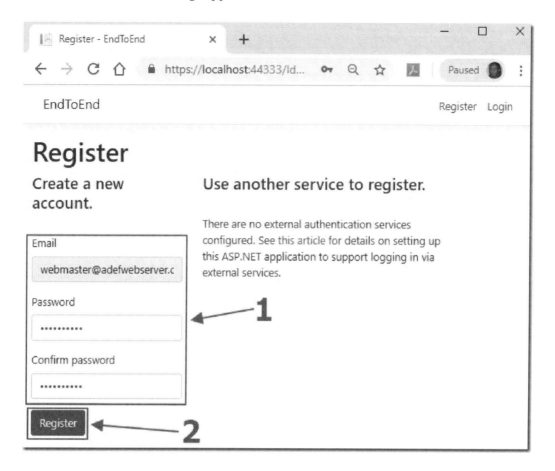

Enter the information to create a **new account**.

Click the **Register** button.

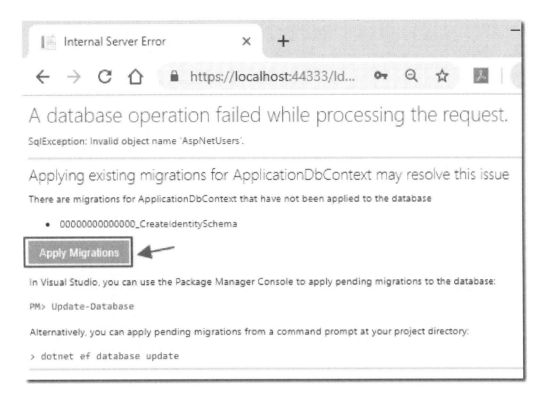

Because this is the first time the database is being used, you will see a message asking you to run the **migration scripts** that will create the database objects needed to support the user membership code.

Click the **Apply Migrations** button.

An Introduction to Building Applications with Blazor

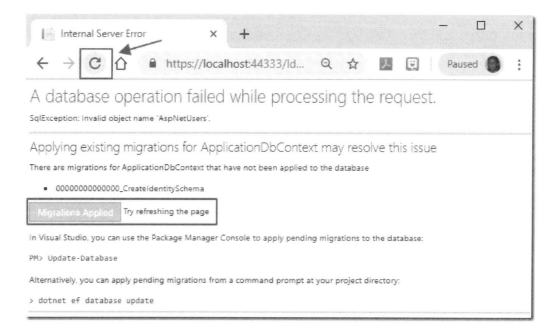

After the message changes to *Migrations Applied*, *refresh* the page in the web browser.

You will now be *logged into* the application.

You can click around the application and see that it works.

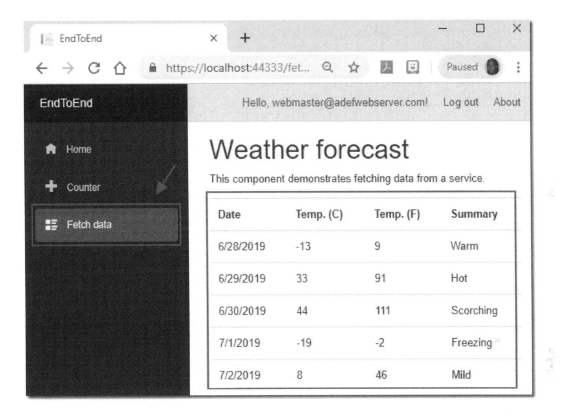

The **Fetch data** page currently shows random data. We will alter the application to allow us to **add, update**, and **delete** this data in the database.

Close the **web browser** to **stop** the application.

Add a Table to the Database

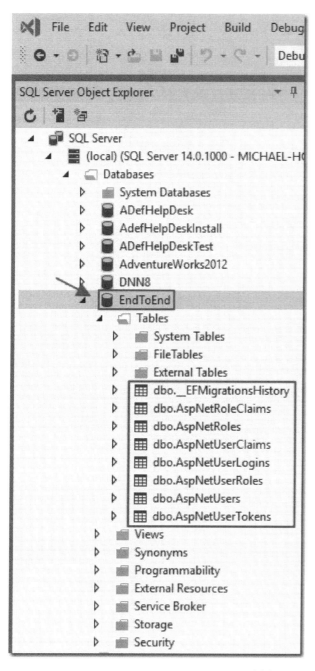

When we return to **Visual Studio** and the **SQL Server Object Explorer** window, we see the **tables** that the *migration scripts* added.

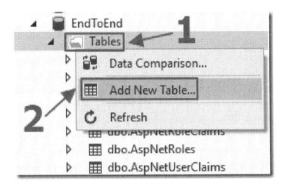

Right-click on the **Tables** node and select **Add New Table**.

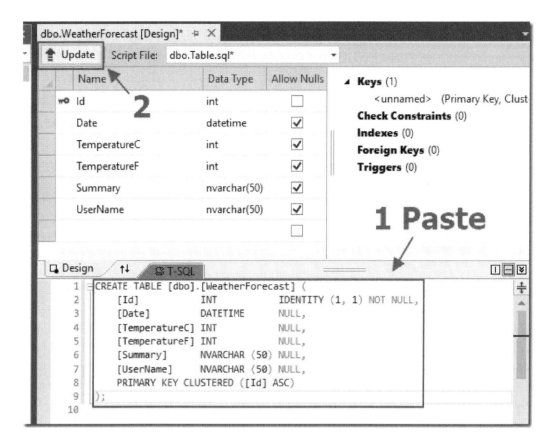

Paste the following script in the **T-SQL** window and then click the **Update** button:

```
CREATE TABLE [dbo].[WeatherForecast] (
    [Id]            INT             IDENTITY (1, 1) NOT NULL,
    [Date]          DATETIME        NULL,
    [TemperatureC]  INT             NULL,
    [TemperatureF]  INT             NULL,
    [Summary]       NVARCHAR (50)   NULL,
    [UserName]      NVARCHAR (50)   NULL,
    PRIMARY KEY CLUSTERED ([Id] ASC)
);
```

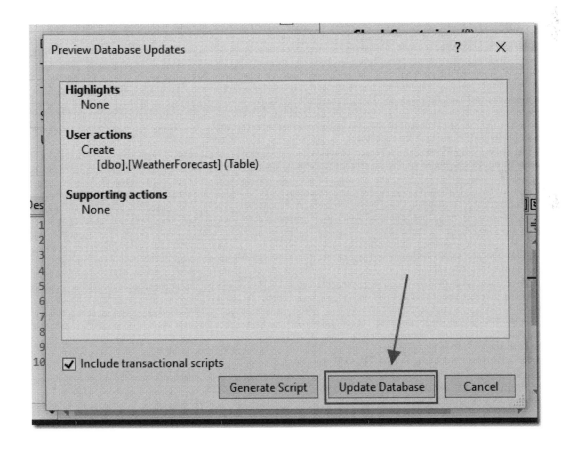

The script will *prepare*.

Click the **Update Database** button.

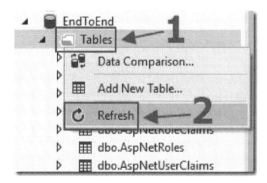

Back in the **Server Explorer** window, *right-click* on **Tables** and select **Refresh**.

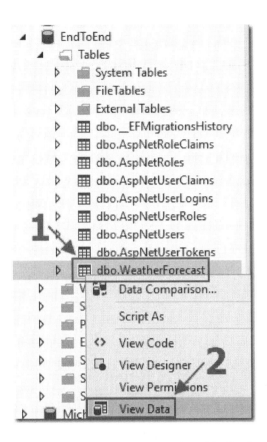

The **WeatherForecast** table will display.

Right-click on the table and select **Show Table Data**.

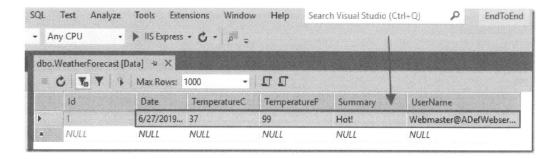

We will enter some **sample data** so that we will be able to **test** the data connection in the next steps.

Set the **UserName** field to the **username** of the **user** that we **registered** an account for earlier.

Create the Data Context

If you do not already have it installed, install **EF Core Power Tools** from:

https://marketplace.visualstudio.com/items?itemName=ErikEJ.EFCorePowerTools

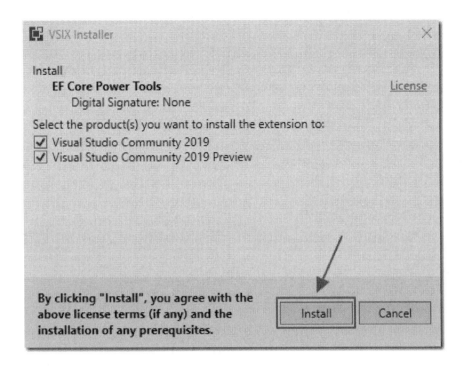

(Note: Before installing, close **Visual Studio**)

(Note: Please give this project a 5-star review on **marketplace.visualstudio.com!**)

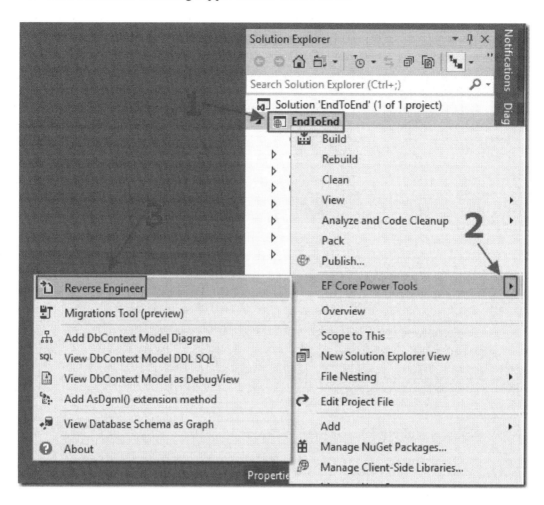

Right-click on the project node in the Solution Explorer and select EF Core Power Tools, then Reverse Engineer.

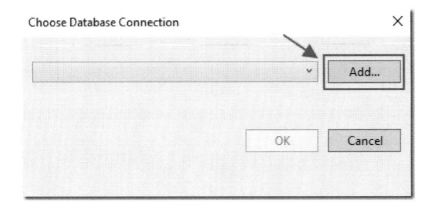

Click the **Add** button.

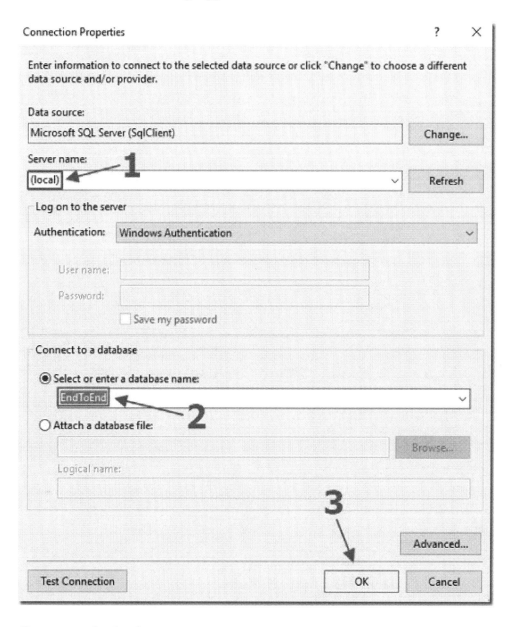

Connect to the database.

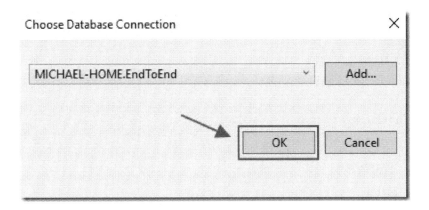

Select the database connection in the **dropdown** and click **OK**.

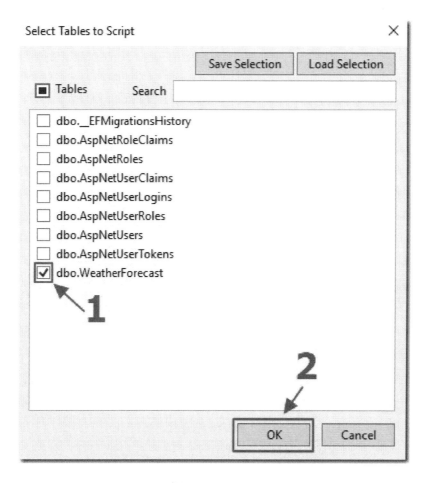

Select the **WeatherForecast** table and click **OK**.

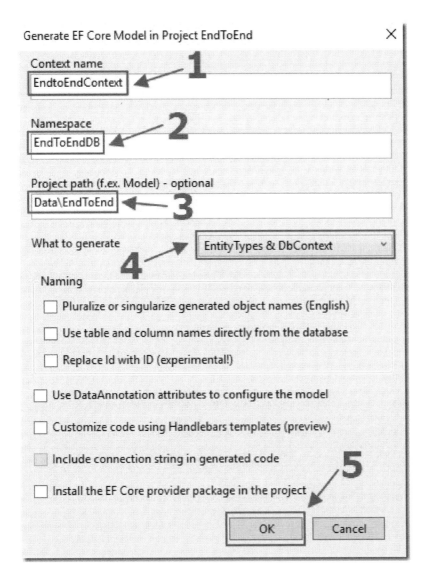

Set the values and click **OK**.

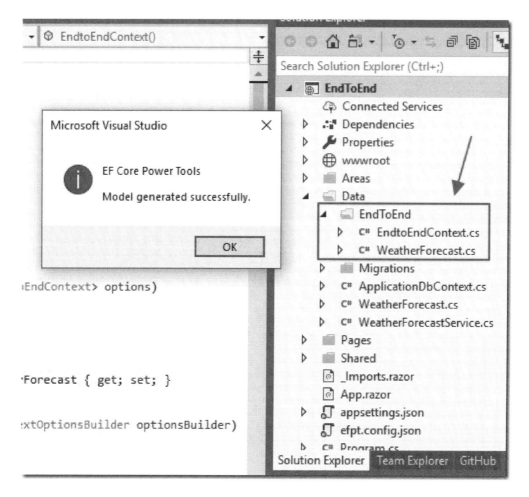

In the **Solution Explorer,** you will see the **Data Context** has been created.

Click the **OK** button to *close* the popup.

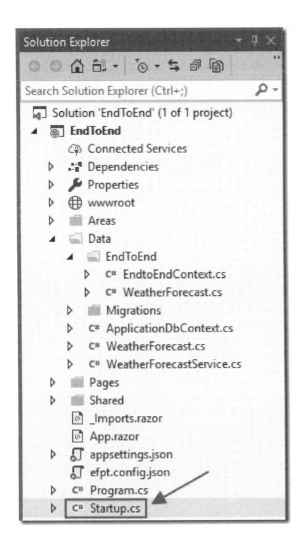

Open the **Startup.cs** file.

Add the following code to the **ConfigureServices** section:

```
// Read the connection string from the appsettings.json file
// Set the database connection for the EndtoEndContext
services.AddDbContext<EndToEndDB.Data.EndToEnd.EndtoEndContext>(options =>
options.UseSqlServer(
    Configuration.GetConnectionString("DefaultConnection")));
```

Also, change this line:

```
services.AddSingleton<WeatherForecastService>();
```

To this:

```
// Scoped creates an instance for each user
services.AddScoped<WeatherForecastService>();
```

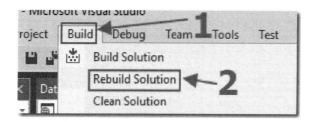

Save the file.

Select **Build,** then **Rebuild Solution.**

Read from the Database

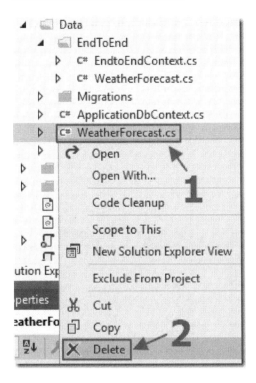

Delete the **Data/WeatherForecast.cs** file in the project.

We will use the **Data/EndToEnd/WeatherForcast.cs** class file created by the **EF Core Tools** instead.

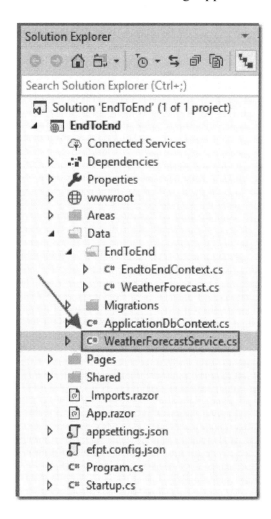

Open the **WeatherForecastService.cs** file.

Replace **all** the code with the following code:

```
using EndToEndDB.Data.EndToEnd;
using System.Collections.Generic;
using System.Linq;
using System.Threading.Tasks;
namespace EndToEnd.Data
{
    public class WeatherForecastService
    {
        private readonly EndtoEndContext _context;
        public WeatherForecastService(EndtoEndContext context)
        {
            _context = context;
        }
        public Task<List<WeatherForecast>>
            GetForecastAsync(string strCurrentUser)
        {
        List<WeatherForecast> colWeatherForcasts =
            new List<WeatherForecast>();
        // Get Weather Forecasts
        colWeatherForcasts =
            (from weatherForecast in _context.WeatherForecast
                // only get entries for the current logged in user
                where weatherForecast.UserName == strCurrentUser
            select weatherForecast).ToList();
        return Task.FromResult(colWeatherForcasts);
        }
    }
}
```

This:

```
private readonly EndtoEndContext _context;
public WeatherForecastService(EndtoEndContext context)
{
    _context = context;
}
```

Connects to the database using the *datacontext* we created with the **EF Core tools**.

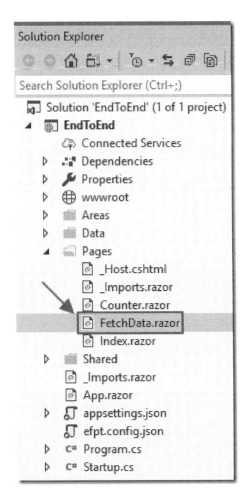

Finally, open the **FetchData.razor** file.

Replace all the code with the following code:

```
@page "/fetchdata"
@using EndToEnd.Data
@using EndToEndDB.Data.EndToEnd
@inject AuthenticationStateProvider AuthenticationStateProvider
@*
    Using OwningComponentBase ensures that the service and related services
    that share its scope are disposed with the component.
    Otherwise DbContext in ForecastService will live for the life of the
    connection, which may be problematic if clients stay
    connected for a long time.
    We access WeatherForecastService using @Service
*@
@inherits OwningComponentBase<WeatherForecastService>
<h1>Weather forecast</h1>
<!-- AuthorizeView allows us to only show sections of the page -->
<!-- based on the security on the current user -->
<AuthorizeView>
    <!-- Show this section if the user is logged in -->
    <Authorized>
        <h4>Hello, @context.User.Identity.Name!</h4>
        @if (forecasts == null)
        {
            <!-- Show this if the current user has no data... yet... -->
            <p><em>Loading...</em></p>
        }
        else
        {
            <!-- Show the forecasts for the current user -->
            <table class="table">
                <thead>
                    <tr>
                        <th>Date</th>
                        <th>Temp. (C)</th>
                        <th>Temp. (F)</th>
                        <th>Summary</th>
                    </tr>
                </thead>
                <tbody>
                    @foreach (var forecast in forecasts)
                    {
                        <tr>
                            <td>@forecast.Date.Value.ToShortDateString()</td>
                            <td>@forecast.TemperatureC</td>
                            <td>@forecast.TemperatureF</td>
                            <td>@forecast.Summary</td>
                        </tr>
                    }
                </tbody>
            </table>
        }
    </Authorized>
    <!-- Show this section if the user is not logged in -->
    <NotAuthorized>
        <p>You're not signed in.</p>
    </NotAuthorized>
</AuthorizeView>
```

134

```
@code {
    // AuthenticationState is available as a CascadingParameter
    [CascadingParameter]
    private Task<AuthenticationState> authenticationStateTask { get; set; }
    List<WeatherForecast> forecasts;
    protected override async Task OnInitializedAsync()
    {
        // Get the current user
        var user = (await authenticationStateTask).User;
        // Get the forecasts for the current user
        // We access WeatherForecastService using @Service
        forecasts = await @Service.GetForecastAsync(user.Identity.Name);
    }
}
```

This code simply calls the **GetForecastAsync** method we created in the previous step, passing the **username** of the currently *logged in user*.

In a normal web application, we would have to make an *http web* call from this *client code* to the code that connects to the database.

With **server-side Blazor,** we don't have to do that, yet the call is still *secure* because the code is rendered on the *server*.

Build and run the project.

If we are not logged in and we go to the **Fetch data** page, we will see a message indicating we are *not signed in*.

Click the **Login** button.

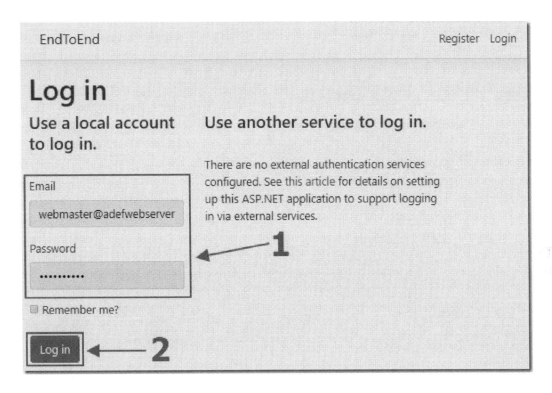

Log in as the user we created data for earlier.

After you are logged in, switch to the **Fetch data** page and you will see the data for the user we entered earlier.

Inserting Data into the Database

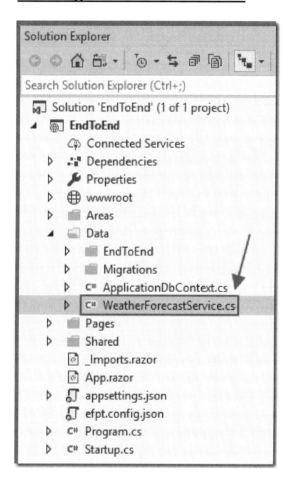

Open the **WeatherForecastService.cs** file and *add* the following method:

```
public Task<WeatherForecast>
    CreateForecastAsync(WeatherForecast objWeatherForecast)
{
    _context.WeatherForecast.Add(objWeatherForecast);
    _context.SaveChanges();
    return Task.FromResult(objWeatherForecast);
}
```

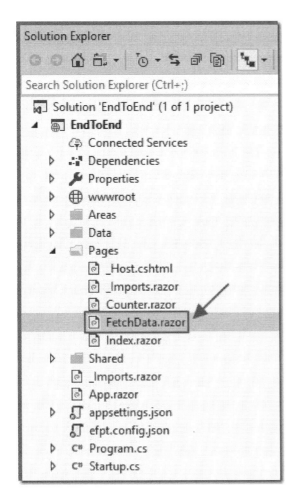

An Introduction to Building Applications with Blazor

Open the **FetchData.razor** file.

Add the following **HTML markup** directly under the existing *table* element:

```
<p>
    <!-- Add a new forecast -->
    <button class="btn btn-primary"
            @onclick="AddNewForecast">
        Add New Forecast
    </button>
</p>
```

This adds a **button** to allow a new *forecast* to be added.

Add the following code below the previous code:

```razor
@if (ShowPopup)
{
    <!-- This is the popup to create or edit a forecast -->
    <div class="modal" tabindex="-1" style="display:block" role="dialog">
        <div class="modal-dialog">
            <div class="modal-content">
                <div class="modal-header">
                    <h3 class="modal-title">Edit Forecast</h3>
                    <!-- Button to close the popup -->
                    <button type="button" class="close"
                            @onclick="ClosePopup">
                        <span aria-hidden="true">X</span>
                    </button>
                </div>
                <!-- Edit form for the current forecast -->
                <div class="modal-body">
                    <input class="form-control" type="text"
                           placeholder="Celsius forecast"
                           @bind="objWeatherForecast.TemperatureC" />
                    <input class="form-control" type="text"
                           placeholder="Fahrenheit forecast"
                           @bind="objWeatherForecast.TemperatureF" />
                    <input class="form-control" type="text"
                           placeholder="Summary"
                           @bind="objWeatherForecast.Summary" />
                    <br />
                    <!-- Button to save the forecast -->
                    <button class="btn btn-primary"
                            @onclick="SaveForecast">
                        Save
                    </button>
                </div>
            </div>
        </div>
    </div>
}
```

This adds a form (that will be displayed as a *popup* because the class for the DIV

141

is *modal*) that allows the user to enter (and later *edit*) data for a forecast.

We do not need *JavaScript* to make this **popup** show. We only need to wrap this code with:

```
@if (ShowPopup)
{
    ...
}
```

When the **ShowPopup** value is *true* the **popup** will show. When the value is *false*, the **popup** will disappear.

Add the following code to the @code section:

```csharp
WeatherForecast objWeatherForecast = new WeatherForecast();
bool ShowPopup = false;
void ClosePopup()
{
    // Close the Popup
    ShowPopup = false;
}
void AddNewForecast()
{
    // Make new forecast
    objWeatherForecast = new WeatherForecast();
    // Set Id to 0 so we know it is a new record
    objWeatherForecast.Id = 0;
    // Open the Popup
    ShowPopup = true;
}
async Task SaveForecast()
{
    // Close the Popup
    ShowPopup = false;
    // Get the current user
    var user = (await authenticationStateTask).User;
    // A new forecast will have the Id set to 0
    if (objWeatherForecast.Id == 0)
    {
        // Create new forecast
        WeatherForecast objNewWeatherForecast = new WeatherForecast();
        objNewWeatherForecast.Date = System.DateTime.Now;
        objNewWeatherForecast.Summary = objWeatherForecast.Summary;
        objNewWeatherForecast.TemperatureC =
        Convert.ToInt32(objWeatherForecast.TemperatureC);
        objNewWeatherForecast.TemperatureF =
        Convert.ToInt32(objWeatherForecast.TemperatureF);
        objNewWeatherForecast.UserName = user.Identity.Name;
        // Save the result
        var result =
        @Service.CreateForecastAsync(objNewWeatherForecast);
    }
    else
    {
        // This is an update
    }
    // Get the forecasts for the current user
    forecasts =
    await @Service.GetForecastAsync(user.Identity.Name);
}
```

When you run the project, you can click the **Add New Forecast** button to *add* an entry.

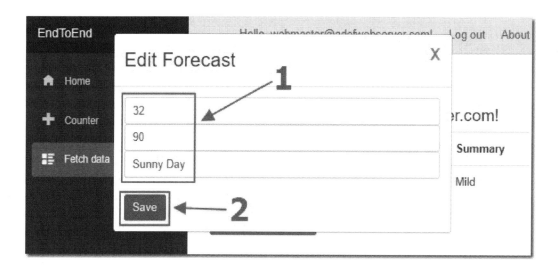

The form only requires a **Fahrenheit, Celsius,** and a **summary**, because the other values (**date** and **username**), will be set by the code.

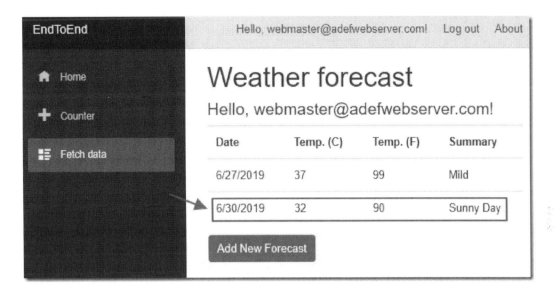

After clicking the **Save** button, the entry is *saved* to the database and displayed.

Updating the Data

Open the **WeatherForecastService.cs** file and *add* the following method:

```csharp
public Task<bool>
    UpdateForecastAsync(WeatherForecast objWeatherForecast)
{
    var ExistingWeatherForecast =
        _context.WeatherForecast
        .Where(x => x.Id == objWeatherForecast.Id)
        .FirstOrDefault();
    if (ExistingWeatherForecast != null)
    {
        ExistingWeatherForecast.Date =
            objWeatherForecast.Date;
        ExistingWeatherForecast.Summary =
            objWeatherForecast.Summary;
        ExistingWeatherForecast.TemperatureC =
            objWeatherForecast.TemperatureC;
        ExistingWeatherForecast.TemperatureF =
            objWeatherForecast.TemperatureF;
        _context.SaveChanges();
    }
    else
    {
        return Task.FromResult(false);
    }
    return Task.FromResult(true);
}
```

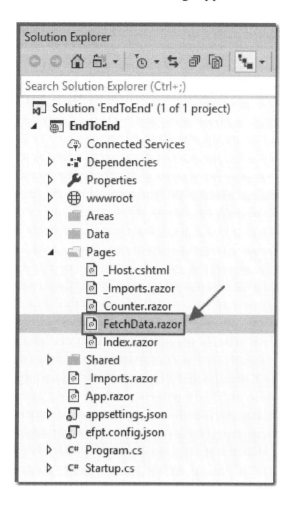

Open the **FetchData.razor** file.

Replace the existing *table* element with the following markup that adds an **edit** button in the last column (that calls the **EditForecast** method we will add in the next step):

```
<table <class="table">
    <thead>
        <tr>
            <th>Date</th>
            <th>Temp. (C)</th>
            <th>Temp. (F)</th>
            <th>Summary</th>
            <th></th>
        </tr>
    </thead>
    <tbody>
        @foreach (var forecast in forecasts)
        {
            <tr>
                <td>@forecast.Date.Value.ToShortDateString()</td>
                <td>@forecast.TemperatureC</td>
                <td>@forecast.TemperatureF</td>
                <td>@forecast.Summary</td>
                <td>
                    <!-- Edit the current forecast -->
                    <button class="btn btn-primary"
                            @onclick="(() => EditForecast(forecast))">
                        Edit
                    </button>
                </td>
            </tr>
        }
    </tbody>
</table>
```

Add the following code to the @code section:

```
void EditForecast(WeatherForecast weatherForecast)
{
    // Set the selected forecast
    // as the current forecast
    objWeatherForecast = weatherForecast;
    // Open the Popup
    ShowPopup = true;
}
```

This sets the current record to the **objWeatherForecast** object that the **popup** is bound to and opens the **popup**.

Finally, change the existing **SaveForecast** method to the following:

```
async Task SaveForecast()
{
    // Close the Popup
    ShowPopup = false;
    // Get the current user
    var user = (await authenticationStateTask).User;
    // A new forecast will have the Id set to 0
    if (objWeatherForecast.Id == 0)
    {
        // Create new forecast
        WeatherForecast objNewWeatherForecast = new WeatherForecast();
        objNewWeatherForecast.Date = System.DateTime.Now;
        objNewWeatherForecast.Summary = objWeatherForecast.Summary;
        objNewWeatherForecast.TemperatureC =
        Convert.ToInt32(objWeatherForecast.TemperatureC);
        objNewWeatherForecast.TemperatureF =
        Convert.ToInt32(objWeatherForecast.TemperatureF);
        objNewWeatherForecast.UserName = user.Identity.Name;
        // Save the result
        var result =
        @Service.CreateForecastAsync(objNewWeatherForecast);
    }
    else
    {
        // This is an update
        var result =
        @Service.UpdateForecastAsync(objWeatherForecast);
    }
    // Get the forecasts for the current user
    forecasts =
    await @Service.GetForecastAsync(user.Identity.Name);
}
```

This simply adds one line:

```
// This is an update
var result =
@Service.UpdateForecastAsync(objWeatherForecast);
```

To the existing method to handle an *update* rather than an *insert*.

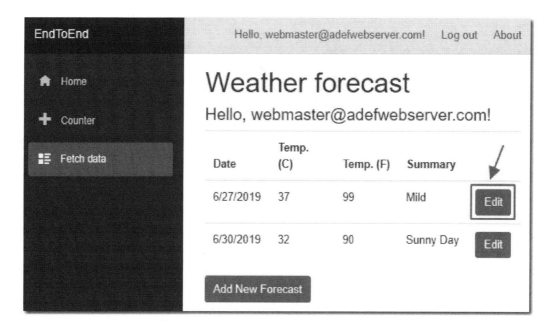

When we run the application, we now have an **Edit** button to *edit* the existing record.

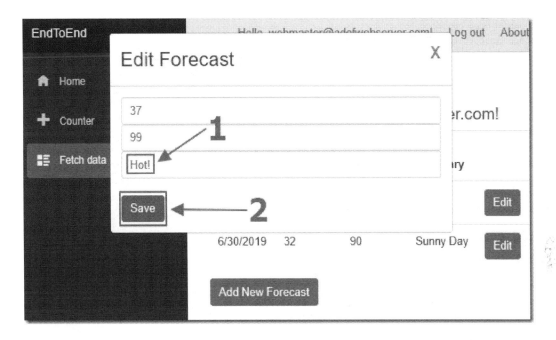

The existing record will display in the **popup**, allowing us to *edit* the data and *save* it.

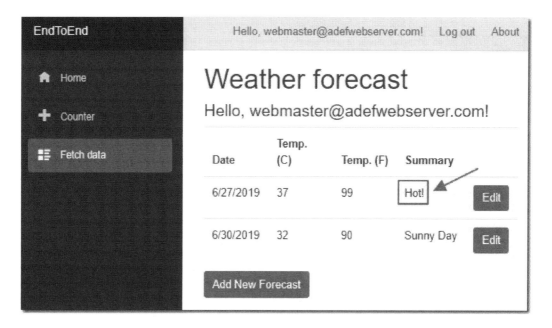

The updated record is then displayed in the table.

Deleting the Data

Open the **WeatherForecastService.cs** file and *add* the following method:

```
public Task<bool>
    DeleteForecastAsync(WeatherForecast objWeatherForecast)
{
    var ExistingWeatherForecast =
        _context.WeatherForecast
        .Where(x => x.Id == objWeatherForecast.Id)
        .FirstOrDefault();
    if (ExistingWeatherForecast != null)
    {
        _context.WeatherForecast.Remove(ExistingWeatherForecast);
        _context.SaveChanges();
    }
    else
    {
        return Task.FromResult(false);
    }
    return Task.FromResult(true);
}
```

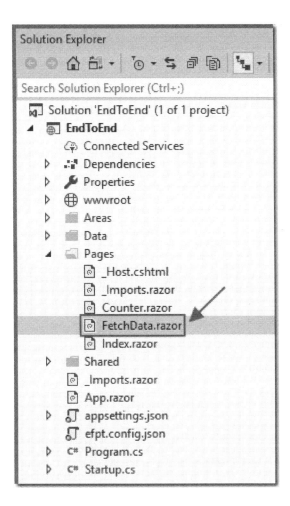

Open the **FetchData.razor** file.

Add code markup for a **Delete** button under the code markup for the current **Save** button in the **popup**:

```
<!-- Only show delete button if not a new record -->
@if (objWeatherForecast.Id > 0)
{
    <!-- Button to delete the forecast -->
    <button class="btn btn-primary"
            @onclick="DeleteForecast">
        Delete
    </button>
}
```

Add the following code to the @code section:

```
async Task DeleteForecast()
{
    // Close the Popup
    ShowPopup = false;
    // Get the current user
    var user = (await authenticationStateTask).User;
    // Delete the forecast
    var result = @Service.DeleteForecastAsync(objWeatherForecast);
    // Get the forecasts for the current user
    forecasts =
    await @Service.GetForecastAsync(user.Identity.Name);
}
```

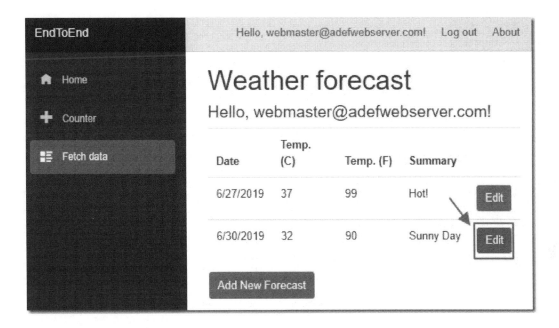

When we run the code and click the **Edit** button…

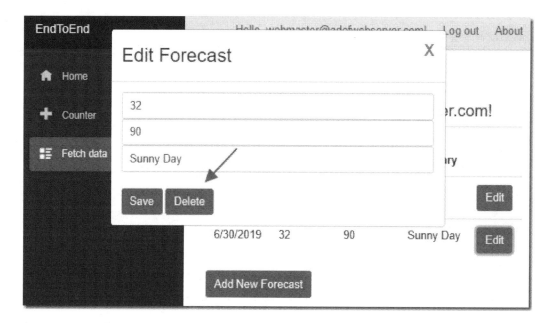

… we now see a **Delete** button that will *delete* the record.

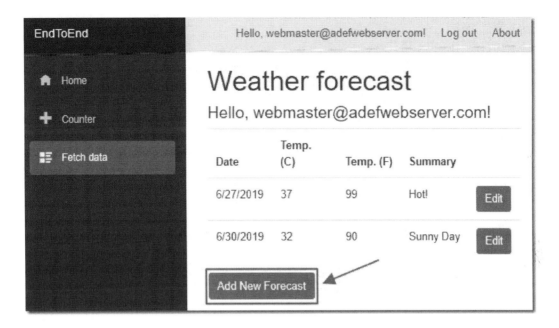

However, when we *click* the **Add New Forecast** button that opens the same **popup**…

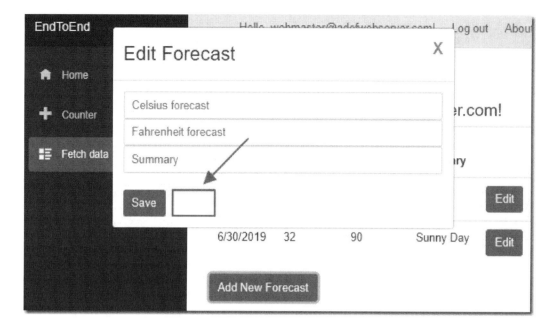

The **delete button** does not display (because there is no record to delete at this point).

Chapter 5: Blazor Forms and Validation

The sample code for this chapter can be obtained at the link "Blazor Forms and Validation" at http://BlazorHelpWebsite.com/Downloads.aspx

Microsoft **Blazor** allows you to easily create **forms** with **validation** to collect data.

We will start with the project created in the previous chapter: **Creating A Step-By-Step End-To-End Database Server-Side Blazor Application**.

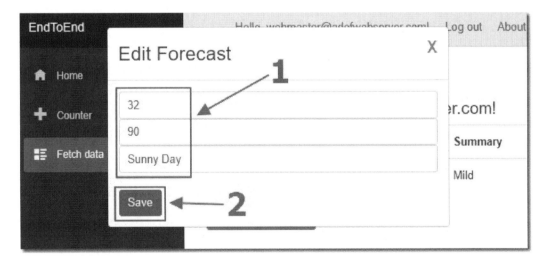

That project presents a **form** that allows you to *insert* and *update* data, but it currently provides no **validation** for the data entered.

We will create a **form** that will *validate* each **field**.

In addition, we will demonstrate validation of **date**, **integer**, and **dropdown** controls.

Add Data Annotations

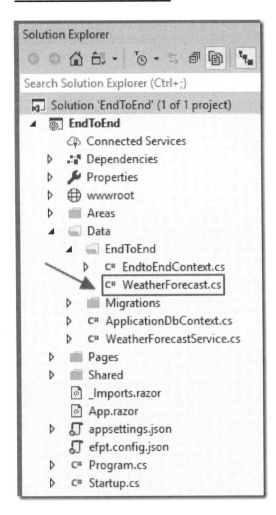

Validation in **Blazor** is implemented by *decorating properties* in a **class** with **data annotations**.

Open the **EndToEnd** project, from the previous chapter, in **Visual Studio**, and open the **WeatherForecast** class, and change *all the code* from this:

```
using System;
using System.Collections.Generic;
namespace EndToEndDB.Data.EndToEnd
{
    public partial class WeatherForecast
    {
        public int Id { get; set; }
        public DateTime? Date { get; set; }
        public int? TemperatureC { get; set; }
        public int? TemperatureF { get; set; }
        public string Summary { get; set; }
        public string UserName { get; set; }
    }
}
```

to this:

```csharp
using System;
using System.ComponentModel.DataAnnotations;
namespace EndToEndDB.Data.EndToEnd
{
    public partial class WeatherForecast
    {
        public int Id { get; set; }
        [Required]
        public DateTime? Date { get; set; }
        [Required(ErrorMessage =
            "Celsius is required")]
        [Range(typeof(int), "-51", "106",
            ErrorMessage =
            "Enter a valid Celsius range (-51 to 106).")]
        public int? TemperatureC { get; set; }
        [Required(ErrorMessage =
            "Fahrenheit is required")]
        [Range(typeof(int), "-60", "224",
            ErrorMessage =
            "Enter a valid Fahrenheit range (-60 to 224).")]
        public int? TemperatureF { get; set; }
        [Required]
        [StringLength(50, MinimumLength = 2,
            ErrorMessage =
            "Summary must be set and maximum of 50 characters.")]
        public string Summary { get; set; }
        public string UserName { get; set; }
    }
    // This class will hold the possible options that
    // will be displayed on the dropdown for the Summary property
    public partial class WeatherForecastOptions
    {
        public string OptionName { get; set; }
        public string OptionValue { get; set; }
    }
}
```

The *data annotations* will control the **validation**.

The **form validation controls**, added later, will simply **trigger** and **display** the results of these *validation* rules.

Add the Form Validation Controls

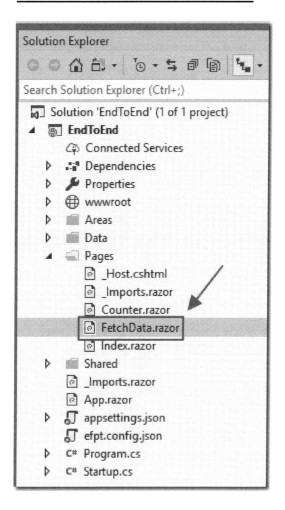

Open the **FetchData.razor** page.

Change the code for the **Save** button from this:

```
<!-- Button to save the forecast -->
<button class="btn btn-primary"
        @onclick="SaveForecast">
    Save
</button>
```

To This:

```
<!-- Button to save the forecast -->
<button class="btn btn-primary"
        type="submit">
    Save
</button>
```

The **Save** button will now only trigger a ***form submit*** (and no longer call the **SaveForecast** method directly).

We then *wrap* the existing **form controls** in an **EditForm** control that is bound to an *instance* of the **WeatherForcast** class that we decorated with the **validation rules**.

We set the **Context** property to *formContext* (any *alias name* will work) because

169

this **EditForm** is contained in an **AuthorizeView** control, and we would otherwise get *build errors* because the **default name** of the **context** for both controls is *"context,"* and this would cause an *ambiguity*.

We would see an error like the following:

> CS0136   A local or parameter named 'context' cannot be declared in this scope because that name is used in an enclosing local scope to define a local or parameter

We also set the **OnValidSubmit** property to call the **SaveForecast** method after the *form data* has passed all *validations*.

```
<!-- Edit form for the current forecast -->
<EditForm Context="formContext"
          Model="objWeatherForecast"
          OnValidSubmit="SaveForecast">
    // Existing Form code goes here...
</EditForm>
```

We add the **validation controls**:

```
<!-- This will validate the form -->
<DataAnnotationsValidator />
<!-- This will show any validation errors -->
<ValidationSummary />
```

Finally, we *update* the **form controls** to the following:

```
<p>
    <label for="Date">Date: </label>
    <InputDate id="Date" class="form-control"
                placeholder="Date"
                @bind-Value="objWeatherForecast.Date" />
</p><p>
    <label for="TemperatureC">Celsius: </label>
    <InputNumber id="TemperatureC" class="form-control"
                placeholder="Celsius forecast"
                @bind-Value="objWeatherForecast.TemperatureC" />
</p><p>
    <label for="TemperatureF">Fahrenheit: </label>
    <InputNumber id="TemperatureF" class="form-control"
                placeholder="Fahrenheit forecast"
                @bind-Value="objWeatherForecast.TemperatureF" />
</p><p>
    <label for="Summary">Summary: </label>
    <InputText id="Summary" class="form-control"
                placeholder="Summary forecast"
                @bind-Value="objWeatherForecast.Summary" />
</p>
```

Essentially, we use an **InputDate** control for the **date** field, an **InputText** control for the **Summary** text field, and **InputNumber** controls for the **integer** fields.

The complete **EditForm** code is indicated below:

```
<!-- Edit form for the current forecast -->
<EditForm Context="formContext"
          Model="objWeatherForecast"
          OnValidSubmit="SaveForecast">
    <!-- This will validate the form -->
    <DataAnnotationsValidator />
    <!-- This will show any validation errors -->
    <ValidationSummary />
    <div class="modal-body">
        <p>
            <label for="Date">Date: </label>
            <InputDate id="Date" class="form-control"
                       placeholder="Date"
                       @bind-Value="objWeatherForecast.Date" />
        </p><p>
            <label for="TemperatureC">Celsius: </label>
            <InputNumber id="TemperatureC" class="form-control"
                         placeholder="Celsius forecast"
                         @bind-Value="objWeatherForecast.TemperatureC" />
        </p><p>
            <label for="TemperatureF">Fahrenheit: </label>
            <InputNumber id="TemperatureF" class="form-control"
                         placeholder="Fahrenheit forecast"
                         @bind-Value="objWeatherForecast.TemperatureF" />
        </p><p>
            <label for="Summary">Summary: </label>
            <InputText id="Summary" class="form-control"
                       placeholder="Summary forecast"
                       @bind-Value="objWeatherForecast.Summary" />
        </p>
        <br />
        <!-- Button to save the forecast -->
        <button class="btn btn-primary"
                type="submit">
            Save
        </button>
        <!-- Only show delete button if not a new record -->
        @if (objWeatherForecast.Id > 0)
        {
            <!-- Button to delete the forecast -->
            <button class="btn btn-primary"
                    @onclick="DeleteForecast">
                Delete
            </button>
        }
    </div>
</EditForm>
```

We can *run* the application, *log in*, *navigate* to the **Fetch data** page, and click the **Add New Forecast** button…

…this will open the **EditForm** control in a **popup**.

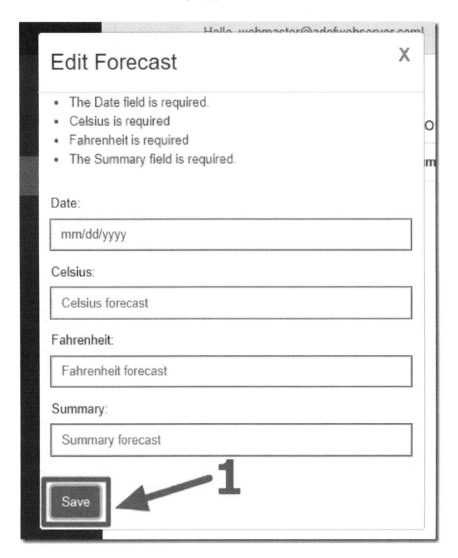

If we don't enter any data, and try to *submit* the form, we see that the **validation rules**, that we added earlier, will be *enforced*.

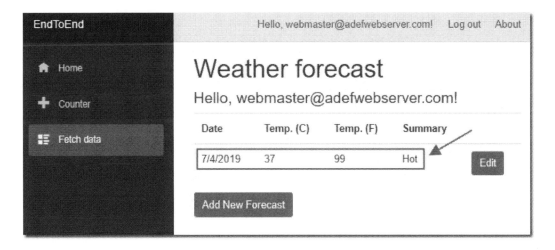

When we enter *valid data*, the **popup** will *close* and the data will be *saved*.

Validate a Dropdown Control

To demonstrate adding **validation** to a *dropdown control*, we will convert the **Summary** field to a *dropdown*.

In the @code section of the **FetchData.razor** page, add the following code:

```
List<WeatherForecastOptions> SummaryOptions = new List<WeatherForecastOptions>() {
new WeatherForecastOptions() { OptionName = "Select...", OptionValue = " " },
    new WeatherForecastOptions() { OptionName = "Hot", OptionValue = "Hot" },
    new WeatherForecastOptions() { OptionName = "Mild", OptionValue = "Mild" },
    new WeatherForecastOptions() { OptionName = "Cold", OptionValue = "Cold" }};
```

This will create a **SummaryOptions** collection that we will bind to the *dropdown.*

Change the existing **Summary** control (and *label* control) to the following:

```
<label for="Summary">Summary: </label>
<InputSelect id="Summary" class="form-control"
                @bind-Value="objWeatherForecast.Summary">
    @foreach (var option in SummaryOptions)
    {
        <option value="@option.OptionValue">
            @option.OptionName
        </option>
    }
</InputSelect>
```

We are now using an **InputSelect** control that will display as a *dropdown.*

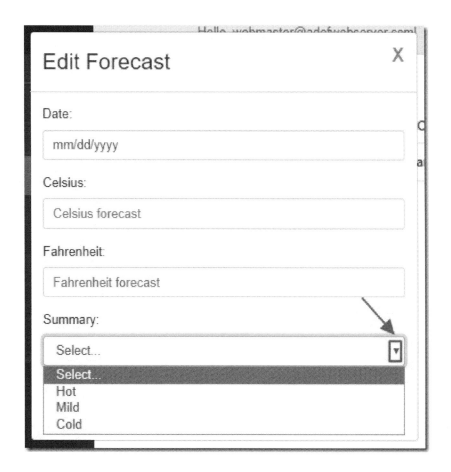

When we run the application, we see that the **Summary** field is now a *dropdown*.

We see that if we do not select an **option** and try to *save*, the *validation* will be enforced.

Customizing Validation

We can use the **ValidationMessage** control to add code such as this, below the **InputSelect** control we just added, to display *validation messages*:

```
<ValidationMessage For="@(() => objWeatherForecast.Summary)" />
```

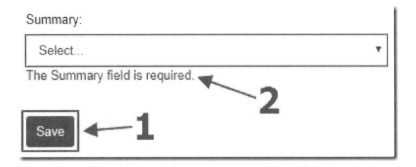

This will cause the *validation* for a single control to be *displayed*.

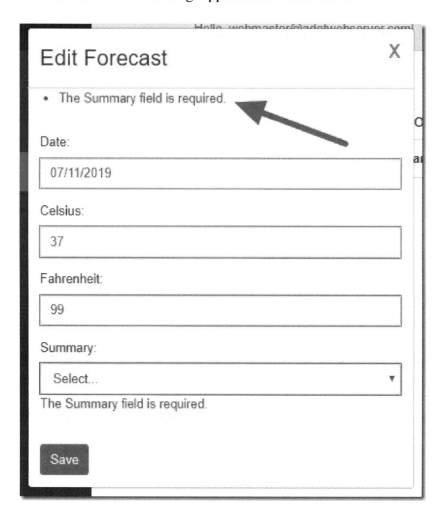

However, the *validation* will also be displayed by the **ValidationSummary** control.

To correct this, we can remove the **ValidationSummary** from the page, and *replace* it with code such as the following, which *iterates through the validation errors* and allows us to **suppress** any we don't want to show:

```
<!-- This will show any validation errors -->
@*<ValidationSummary />*@
<ul class="validation-errors">
    @foreach (
        var message in formContext.GetValidationMessages()
        .Where(x => !x.Contains("Summary")))
    {
        <li class="validation-message">@message</li>
    }
</ul>
```

Now the **Summary** *validation error* appears only once.

Chapter 6: Implementing State Management in Blazor

The sample code for this chapter can be obtained at the link "Implementing State Management In Blazor" at http://BlazorHelpWebsite.com/Downloads.aspx

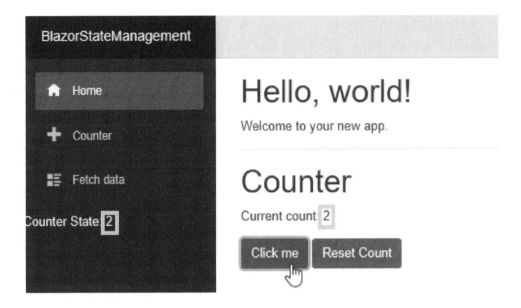

State Management in **Blazor** refers to the technique that you use to *persist data* between **Blazor** pages. Without *state management*, this data would be lost.

In this chapter we will cover the *AppState pattern* that was introduced by the **Microsoft Blazor** team in the **Blazing Pizza workshop** (https://github.com/dotnet-presentations/blazor-workshop).

The Issue – State Is Not Maintained

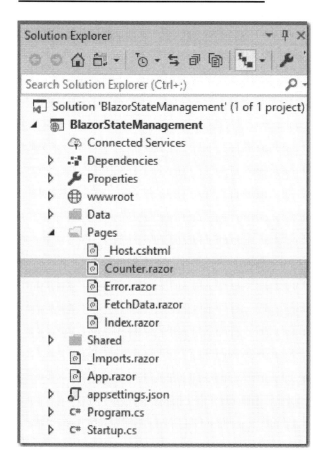

We start off with a **server-side Blazor** application.

We observe the code in the **Counter.razor** control by *running* the application, and *navigating* to that page.

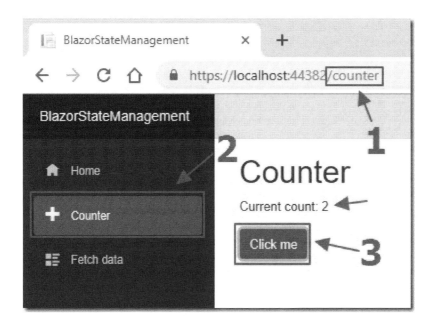

When we *click* the **Click me** button, we see the **Current count** increase.

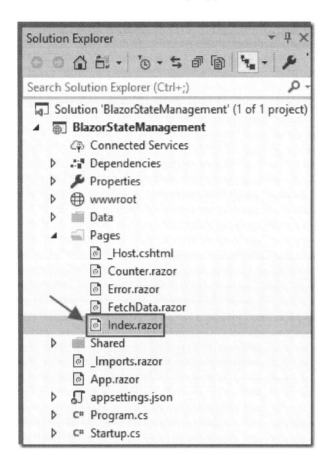

However, if we open the **Index.razor** page and *add* the following code, to add an *instance* of the **Counter** control:

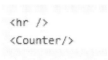

```
<hr />
<Counter/>
```

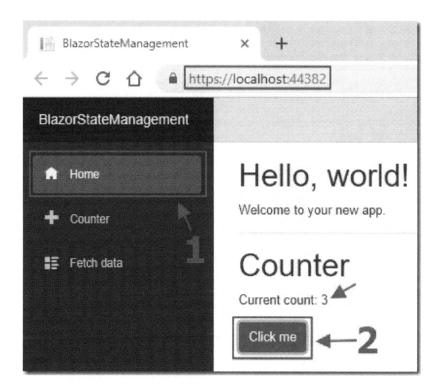

When we *run* the application, we can *increase* the **counter**, by clicking the **Click me** button...

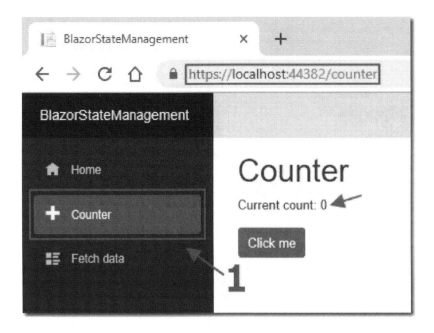

… however, when we *navigate* to the **Counter** page, that *instance* of the **Counter** returns to **0**.

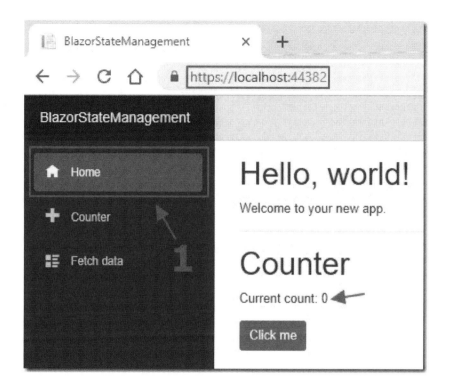

In addition, *returning* to the **Index** page, we see that it will also return the **Current count** to **0**.

Implementing State Management

The first step is to *add* a **class** to hold the **state**.

We *add* a class called **CounterState.cs** using the following code:

```csharp
using System;
using System.Collections.Generic;
using System.Linq;
using System.Threading.Tasks;
namespace BlazorStateManagement
{
    public class CounterState
    {
        public int CurrentCount { get; set; }
    }
}
```

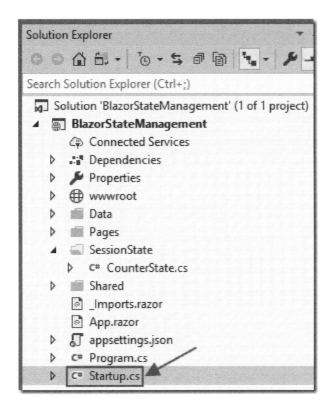

Next, we *register* this class, using *Dependency Injection*, by opening the **Startup.cs** file and *adding* the following code to the end of the **ConfigureServices** method:

```
// ** SESSION STATE
// Singleton usually means for all users,
// where as scoped means for the current unit-of-work
services.AddScoped<CounterState>();
```

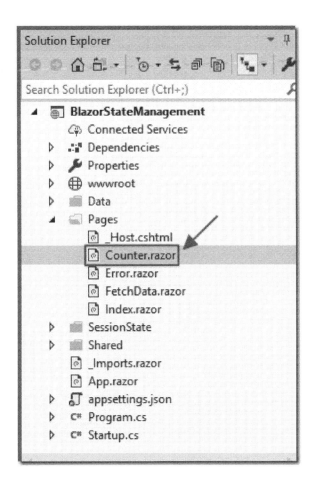

To *consume* the class, we open the **Counter.razor** page and *add* the following code to the top of the code page:

```
@inject CounterState CounterState
```

We change the following code:

```
<p>Current count: @currentCount</p>
```

to:

```
<p>Current count: @CounterState.CurrentCount</p>
```

Finally, we change the code section to the following:

```
@code {
    void IncrementCount()
    {
        // ** SESSION STATE
        int CurrentCount = CounterState.CurrentCount;
        CurrentCount++;
        // Set Current count on the Session State object
        CounterState.CurrentCount = CurrentCount;
    }
}
```

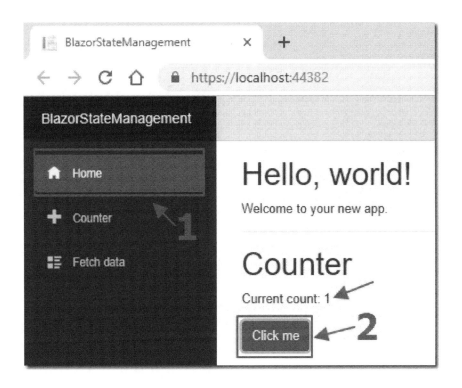

Now, when we *run* the application, we can *increase* the **counter** on the **Index** page…

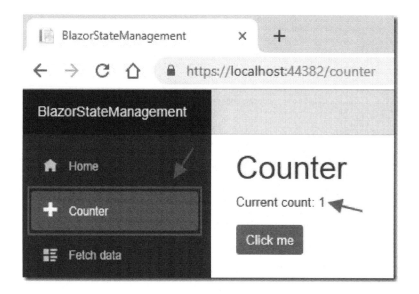

... and the value is *persisted* on the **Counter** page.

Advanced State Management Using EventCallback

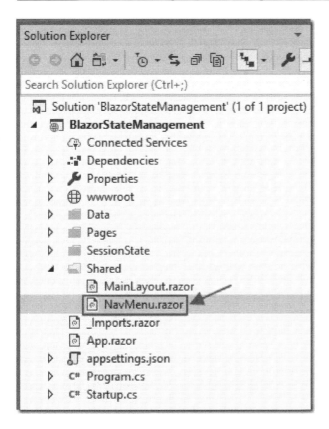

If we open the **NavMenu.razor** file and inject the *state management* class:

```
@inject CounterState CounterState
```

And the following *markup*:

```
<div>
    <p style="color:white">Counter State: @CounterState.CurrentCount</p>
</div>
```

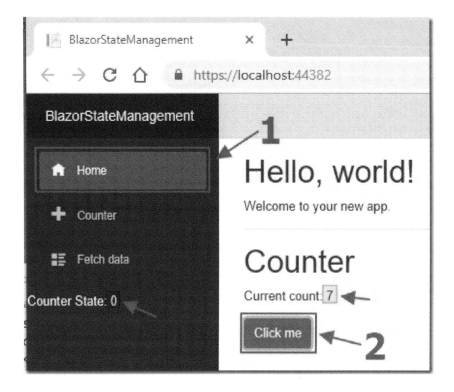

When we *run* the application and *increase* the counter, we see that the count is <u>not</u> increased in the **NavMenu.razor** control…

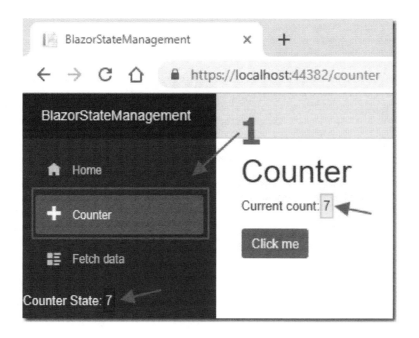

...until we *navigate* to a new page.

Essentially, the *values* in the *state* are being *tracked*, but that value will not necessarily *display* in another control *automatically*.

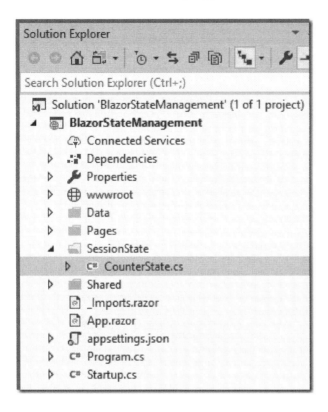

To resolve this, *open* the **CounterState.cs** file and *replace* the code of the **class** with the following code:

```csharp
using System;
public class CounterState
{
    // _currentCount holds the current counter value
    // for the entire application
    private int _currentCount = 0;
    // StateChanged is an event handler other pages
    // can subscribe to
    public event EventHandler StateChanged;
    // This method will always return the current count
    public int GetCurrentCount()
    {
        return _currentCount;
    }
    // This method will be called to update the current count
    public void SetCurrentCount(int paramCount)
    {
        _currentCount = paramCount;
        StateHasChanged();
    }
    // This method will allow us to reset the current count
    public void ResetCurrentCount()
    {
        _currentCount = 0;
        StateHasChanged();
    }
    private void StateHasChanged()
    {
        // This will update any subscribers
        // that the counter state has changed
        // so they can update themselves
        // and show the current counter value
        StateChanged?.Invoke(this, EventArgs.Empty);
    }
}
```

Essentially, we are creating an *Event Handler* that will allow other controls to *subscribe* to it, so that they will be *notified* when *tracked values* change. In addition, we are *adding* **methods** that can be *consumed* and *invoked* by other controls.

This allows us to *centralize state logic code* that is used in multiple places in our application.

Consume the Updated State Management Class

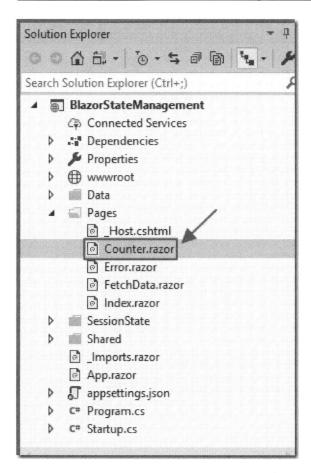

We now need to *update* the existing code to *consume* the updated **State Management** class.

Open the **Counter.razor** control and *change* all the code to the following:

```
@page "/counter"
@inject CounterState CounterState
<h1>Counter</h1>
<!-- We now call the GetCurrentCount() method -->
<!-- to get the current count -->
<p>Current count: @CounterState.GetCurrentCount()</p>
<button class="btn btn-primary"
        @onclick="IncrementCount">
    Click me
</button>
<!-- Add a button to reset the current count -->
<!-- that calls the CounterState class directly -->
<button class="btn btn-primary"
        @onclick="CounterState.ResetCurrentCount">
    Reset Count
</button>
@code {
    void IncrementCount()
    {
        // Call the GetCurrentCount() method
        // to get the current count
        int CurrentCount = CounterState.GetCurrentCount();
        // Increase the count
        CurrentCount++;
        // Set Current count on the Session State object
        CounterState.SetCurrentCount(CurrentCount);
    }
}
```

This demonstrates how a control can *consume* and *invoke* the new **methods** in the **State Management** class.

This control does not need to *subscribe* to the newly added **Event Handler** because this control will update itself *automatically* each time the **button** is clicked to *increase* the **counter**.

However, this is not necessarily true for other controls...

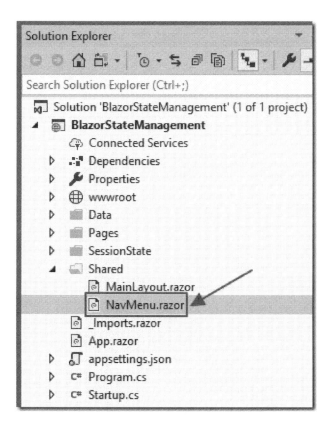

Next, open the **NavMenu.razor** control and change the **DIV**, which displays the **counter state**, to the following:

```
<div>
    <!-- We now call the GetCurrentCount() method -->
    <!-- to get the current count -->
    <p style="color:white">
        Counter State: @CounterState.GetCurrentCount()
    </p>
</div>
```

This will display the latest value of the **counter**; however, it will still not update *automatically*.

We now need to add code to *subscribe* to the **Event Handler** we added to the **State Management** class.

Add the following code to the top of the control:

```
@implements IDisposable
```

This is added because we will add code in the next step that will *properly dispose* of the *subscription* we create, so that we do not have a *memory leak*.

Add the following code to the @code section of the page:

```csharp
// This method is called when the control is initialized
protected override void OnInitialized()
{
    // Subscribe to the StateChanged EventHandler
    CounterState.StateChanged +=
    OnCounterStateAdvancedStateChanged;
}
// This method is fired when the CounterState object
// invokes its StateHasChanged() method
// This will cause this control to invoke its own
// StateHasChanged() method refreshing the page
// and displaying the updated counter value
void OnCounterStateAdvancedStateChanged(
    object sender, EventArgs e) => StateHasChanged();
void IDisposable.Dispose()
{
    // When this control is disposed of
    // unsubscribe from the StateChanged EventHandler
    CounterState.StateChanged -=
    OnCounterStateAdvancedStateChanged;
}
```

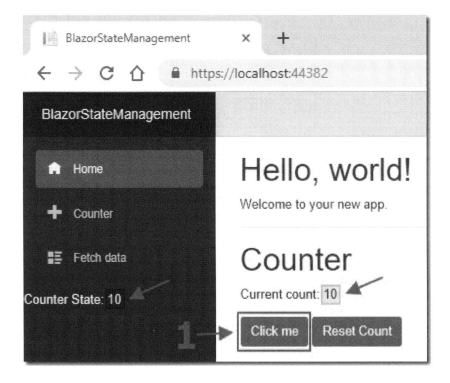

Now, when we *run* the application, the **counter value** is always in *sync*.

We can also now *reset* the **counter** by *clicking* the **Reset Count** button.

Chapter 7: Creating Blazor Templated Components

The sample code for this chapter can be obtained at the link "Creating Blazor Templated Components" at http://BlazorHelpWebsite.com/Downloads.aspx

A **Blazor** application is composed of **components**. These **components** can be made *fully re-usable* by creating **templated components**.

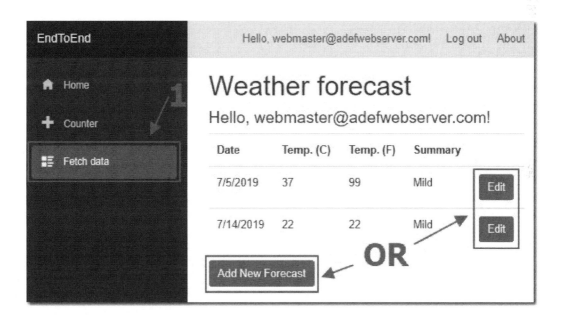

We start with the application created in the code from the previous chapter, **Blazor Forms and Validation**.

In that application, on the **Fetch data** page, if we *click* the **Add New Forecast** button or the **Edit** button next to each row…

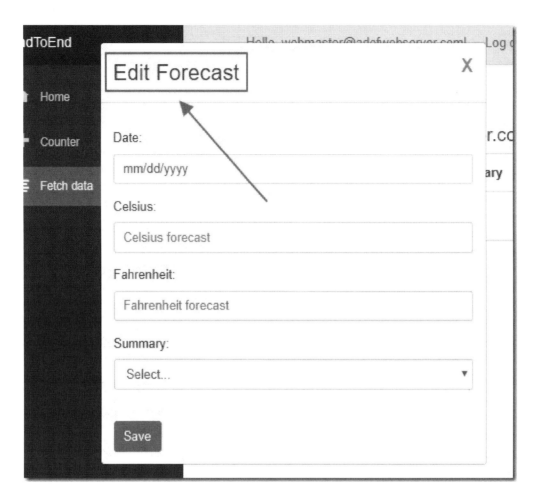

The popup always displays the title **Edit Forecast**.

In this chapter we will create a **Templated control** that will allow us to *replace* the **title** of the **popup dialog**. We will do this not by simply passing a *parameter*, but by *replacing* the **user interface** elements.

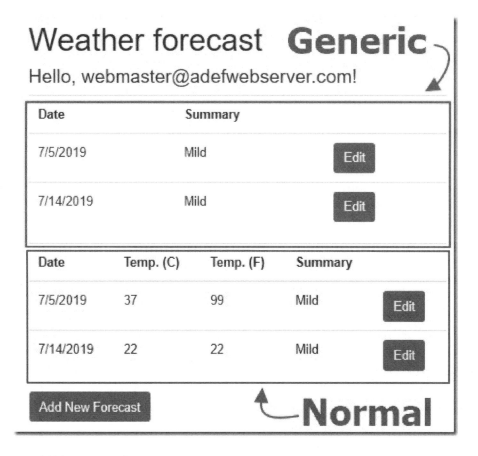

In addition, we will use **Blazor templates** to create a *fully reusable* **generic template control** that can be used with any *data type*.

Create the Dialog Control

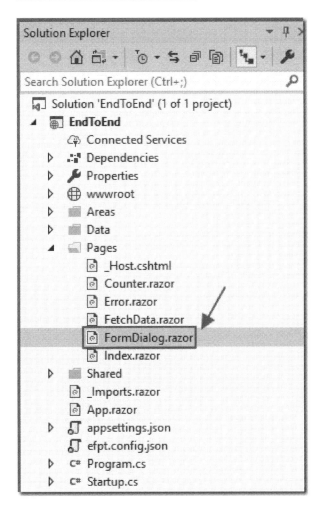

Using the code from the **Blazor Forms and Validation** project, add a new page called **FormDialog.razor,** using the following code:

```
@using EndToEndDB.Data.EndToEnd
@if (Show)
{
    <!-- This is the popup to create or edit a forecast -->
    <div class="modal" tabindex="-1" style="display:block" role="dialog">
        <div class="modal-dialog">
            <div class="modal-content">
                <div class="modal-header">
                    <h3 class="modal-title">Edit Forecast</h3>
                    <!-- Button to close the popup -->
                    <button type="button" class="close"
                            @onclick="ClosePopup">
                        <span aria-hidden="true">X</span>
                    </button>
                </div>
                <!-- Edit form for the current forecast -->
                <EditForm Context="formContext"
                          Model="objWeatherForecast"
                          OnValidSubmit="SaveForecast">
                <!-- This will validate the form -->
                <DataAnnotationsValidator />
                <ul class="validation-errors">
                    @foreach (
                    var message in formContext.GetValidationMessages()
                    .Where(x => !x.Contains("Summary")))
                    {
                        <li class="validation-message">@message</li>
                    }
                </ul>
```

```
                <div class="modal-body">
                    <p>
                        <label for="Date">Date: </label>
                        <InputDate id="Date" class="form-control"
                                   placeholder="Date"
                                   @bind-Value="objWeatherForecast.Date" />
                    </p><p>
                        <label for="TemperatureC">Celsius: </label>
                        <InputNumber id="TemperatureC" class="form-control"
                                     placeholder="Celsius forecast"
                                     @bind-Value="objWeatherForecast.TemperatureC" />
                    </p><p>
                        <label for="TemperatureF">Fahrenheit: </label>
                        <InputNumber id="TemperatureF" class="form-control"
                                     placeholder="Fahrenheit forecast"
                                     @bind-Value="objWeatherForecast.TemperatureF" />
                    </p><p>
                        <label for="Summary">Summary: </label>
                        <InputSelect id="Summary" class="form-control"
                                     @bind-Value="objWeatherForecast.Summary">
                            @foreach (var option in SummaryOptions)
                                {
                                <option value="@option.OptionValue">
                                    @option.OptionName
                                </option>
                                }
                        </InputSelect>
                        <ValidationMessage For="(() => objWeatherForecast.Summary)" />
                    </p>
                    <br />
                    <!-- Button to save the forecast -->
                    <button class="btn btn-primary"
                            type="submit">
                        Save
                    </button>
                    <!-- Only show delete button if not a new record -->
                    @if (objWeatherForecast.Id > 0)
                    {
                        <!-- Button to delete the forecast -->
                        <button class="btn btn-primary"
                                @onclick="DeleteForecast">
                            Delete
                        </button>
                    }
                </div>
            </EditForm>
        </div>
    </div>
</div>
}
```

```
@code {
    [Parameter] public bool Show { get; set; }
    [Parameter] public WeatherForecast objWeatherForecast { get; set; }
    [Parameter] public EventCallback DeleteForecast { get; set; }
    [Parameter] public EventCallback ClosePopup { get; set; }
    [Parameter] public EventCallback SaveForecast { get; set; }
    List<WeatherForecastOptions> SummaryOptions = new List<WeatherForecastOptions>() {
    new WeatherForecastOptions() { OptionName = "Select...", OptionValue = " " },
        new WeatherForecastOptions() { OptionName = "Hot", OptionValue = "Hot" },
        new WeatherForecastOptions() { OptionName = "Mild", OptionValue = "Mild" },
        new WeatherForecastOptions() { OptionName = "Cold", OptionValue = "Cold" }};
}
```

At this point, this is <u>not</u> a **templated component**. It is essentially a copy of the **popup** code from the **FetchData.razor** age.

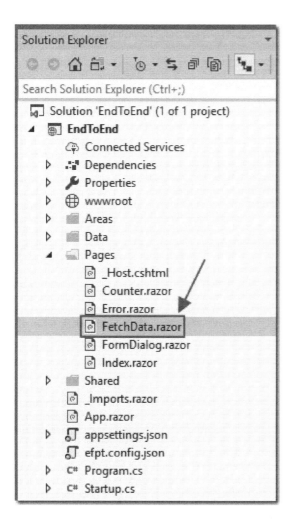

Open the **FetchData.razor** page.

```
FetchData.razor  ⊅ ✕
53  ☐      <p>
54              <!-- Add a new forecast -->
55  ☐          <button class="btn btn-primary"
56                      @onclick="AddNewForecast">          ⌐ Remove
57                  Add New Forecast
58              </button>
59          </p>
60  ☐      @if (ShowPopup)
61          {
62              <!-- This is the popup to create or edit a forecast -->
63  ☐          <div class="modal" tabindex="-1" style="display:block" role="dialog">
64  ☐              <div class="modal-dialog">
65  ☐                  <div class="modal-content">
66  ☐                      <div class="modal-header">
67                              <h3 class="modal-title">Edit Forecast</h3>
68                              <!-- Button to close the popup -->
69  ☐                          <button type="button" class="close"
70                                      @onclick="ClosePopup">
71                                  <span aria-hidden="true">X</span>
72                              </button>
73                          </div>
74                          <!-- Edit form for the current forecast -->
75  ☐                      <EditForm Context="formContext"
76                                  Model="objWeatherForecast"
77                                  OnValidSubmit="SaveForecast">
78
```

Remove the code for the existing **popup**.

Replace with **two instances** of the **dialog component** we just created, one that will be used for creating **new records (ShowNewRecordPopup)** and one for editing **existing records (ShowEditRecordPopup)**.

220

```
<FormDialog Show="ShowNewRecordPopup"
            objWeatherForecast="objWeatherForecast"
            DeleteForecast="DeleteForecast"
            ClosePopup="ClosePopup"
            SaveForecast="SaveForecast">
</FormDialog>
<FormDialog Show="ShowEditRecordPopup"
            objWeatherForecast="objWeatherForecast"
            DeleteForecast="DeleteForecast"
            ClosePopup="ClosePopup"
            SaveForecast="SaveForecast">
</FormDialog>
```

Add variables to pass to the new dialogs to control their display:

```
bool ShowNewRecordPopup = false;
bool ShowEditRecordPopup = false;
```

Change the **ClosePopup()** method to the following code:

```
void ClosePopup()
{
    // Close the Popups
    ShowNewRecordPopup = false;
    ShowEditRecordPopup = false;
}
```

221

Replace all other instances of *ShowPopup* with either *ShowNewRecordPopup* or *ShowEditRecordPopup* depending on the need to show either the **create** or **edit** popup.

For example, change the **EditForecast** method from:

```
void EditForecast(WeatherForecast weatherForecast)
{
    // Set the selected forecast
    // as the current forecast
    objWeatherForecast = weatherForecast;
    // Open the Popup
    ShowPopup = true;
}
```

to:

```
void EditForecast(WeatherForecast weatherForecast)
{
    // Set the selected forecast
    // as the current forecast
    objWeatherForecast = weatherForecast;
    // *** EDIT
    // Open the Popup
    ShowEditRecordPopup = true;
}
```

Change the **AddNewForecast** method to:

```
void AddNewForecast()
{
    // Make new forecast
    objWeatherForecast = new WeatherForecast();
    // Set Id to 0 so we know it is a new record
    objWeatherForecast.Id = 0;
    // *** EDIT
    // Open the Popup
    ShowNewRecordPopup = true;
}
```

An Introduction to Building Applications with Blazor

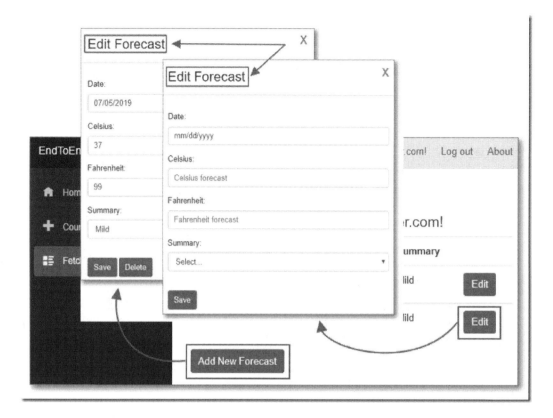

When we *run* the project, the **Add New Forecast** and the **Edit** button still work, but the **title** of the dialog is still the same.

(**Note:** The **Delete** button on the popup is programmatically set to show only when the **record id** is not a *new record* (**objWeatherForecast.Id > 0**)).

Create the Templated Component

A *templated component* is a **Blazor** component that has one or more *parameters* of type **RenderFragment** (or the generic **RenderFragment<T>** demonstrated later).

A **RenderFragment** parameter accepts a **User Interface (UI)** that is then *rendered* by the component. This parameter allows you to fully customize the look and feel of the resulting component while still reusing much of the component structure and logic.

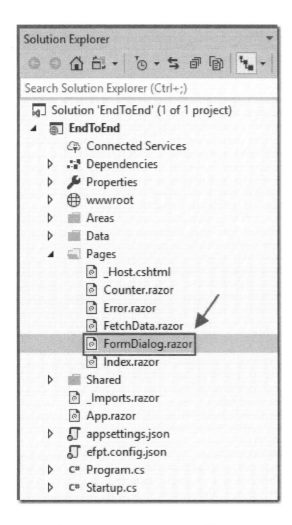

Open the **FormDialog.razor** file.

Add a **RenderFragment** parameter:

```
[Parameter] public RenderFragment HeaderContent { get; set; }
```

Next, to consume the **RenderFragment** parameter, change the following line:

```
<h3 class="modal-title">Edit Forecast</h3>
```

to:

```
@HeaderContent
```

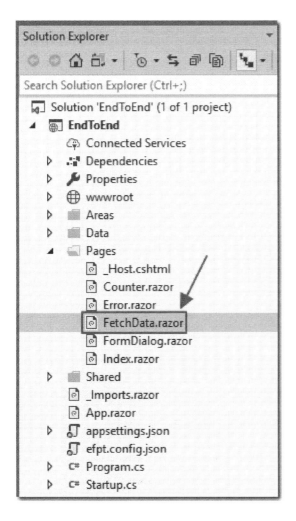

To set the content of the **RenderFragment** parameter, open the **FetchData.razor** page, and change the following code:

```
<FormDialog Show="ShowNewRecordPopup"
            objWeatherForecast="objWeatherForecast"
            DeleteForecast="DeleteForecast"
            ClosePopup="ClosePopup"
            SaveForecast="SaveForecast">
</FormDialog>
<FormDialog Show="ShowEditRecordPopup"
            objWeatherForecast="objWeatherForecast"
            DeleteForecast="DeleteForecast"
            ClosePopup="ClosePopup"
            SaveForecast="SaveForecast">
</FormDialog>
```

to:

```
<FormDialog Show="ShowNewRecordPopup"
            objWeatherForecast="objWeatherForecast"
            DeleteForecast="DeleteForecast"
            ClosePopup="ClosePopup"
            SaveForecast="SaveForecast">
    <HeaderContent>
        <h3 class="modal-title"
            style="color:darkred">
            Create Forecast
        </h3>
    </HeaderContent>
</FormDialog>
<FormDialog Show="ShowEditRecordPopup"
            objWeatherForecast="objWeatherForecast"
            DeleteForecast="DeleteForecast"
            ClosePopup="ClosePopup"
            SaveForecast="SaveForecast">
    <HeaderContent>
        <h3 class="modal-title"
            style="color:darkgreen">
            Edit Forecast
        </h3>
    </HeaderContent>
</FormDialog>
```

```
<FormDialog Show="ShowEditRecordPopup"
            objWeatherForecast="objWeatherForecast"
            DeleteForecast="DeleteForecast"
            ClosePopup="ClosePopup"
            SaveForecast="SaveForecast">
    <HeaderContent>
        <h3 class="modal-title"
            style="color:darkgreen">
            Edit Forecast
        </h3>
    </HeaderContent>
</FormDialog>
```

```
@code {
    [Parameter] public RenderFragment HeaderContent { get; set; }
    [Parameter] public bool Show { get; set; }
    [Parameter] public WeatherForecast objWeatherForecast { get; set; }
    [Parameter] public EventCallback DeleteForecast { get; set; }
    [Parameter] public EventCallback ClosePopup { get; set; }
```

```
@if (Show)
{
    <!-- This is the popup to create or edit a forecast -->
    <div class="modal" tabindex="-1" style="display:block" role="dialog">
        <div class="modal-dialog">
            <div class="modal-content">
                <div class="modal-header">
                    @HeaderContent
                    <!-- Button to close the popup -->
                    <button type="button" class="close"
                            @onclick="ClosePopup">
                        <span aria-hidden="true">X</span>
                    </button>
```

Essentially, we are passing the *content* for the *HeaderContent* **RenderFragment** parameter inside the *HeaderContent* tags.

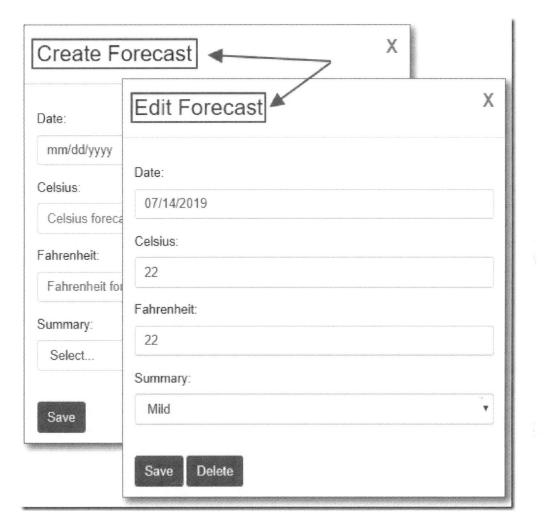

Now, when we *run* the project, each **dialog** will have *customized* header content.

Creating a Generic Templated Component

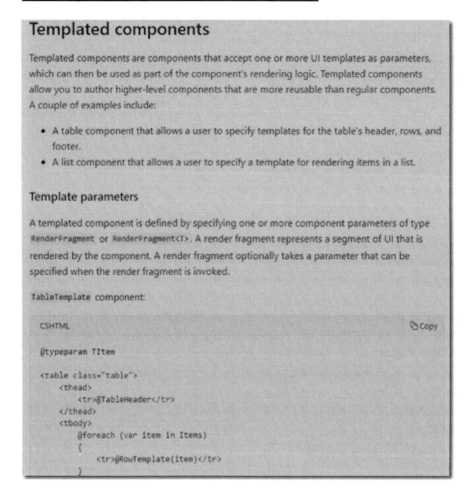

Templated components

Templated components are components that accept one or more UI templates as parameters, which can then be used as part of the component's rendering logic. Templated components allow you to author higher-level components that are more reusable than regular components. A couple of examples include:

- A table component that allows a user to specify templates for the table's header, rows, and footer.
- A list component that allows a user to specify a template for rendering items in a list.

Template parameters

A templated component is defined by specifying one or more component parameters of type `RenderFragment` or `RenderFragment<T>`. A render fragment represents a segment of UI that is rendered by the component. A render fragment optionally takes a parameter that can be specified when the render fragment is invoked.

`TableTemplate` component:

```cshtml
@typeparam TItem

<table class="table">
    <thead>
        <tr>@TableHeader</tr>
    </thead>
    <tbody>
        @foreach (var item in Items)
        {
            <tr>@RowTemplate(item)</tr>
        }
```

In the preceding **templated component** example, the **data type** *always* has to be a type of **WeatherForecast**. However, we can create **templated components** that can work with *any data type*. The data type can be specified at the time the component is consumed.

The **Microsoft Blazor Documentation site** (https://docs.microsoft.com/en-us/aspnet/core/blazor/components?view=aspnetcore-3.0#templated-components) provides an example, using **@typeparam** and **RenderFragment<T>**, to create a *generic template*.

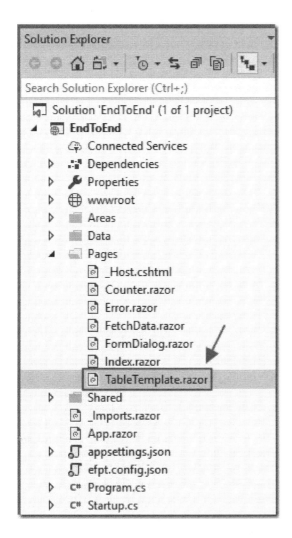

Add a new control called **TableTemplate.razor** using the following code:

```razor
@*To define a generic component*@
@*we use the @typeparam directive to specify *@
@*type parameters*@
@typeparam TItem
@*Create a table*@
<table class="table">
    <thead>
        @*TableHeader will be inserted here*@
        <tr>@TableHeader</tr>
    </thead>
    <tbody>
        @*Items will be iterated at this point*@
        @*Creating a row for each item*@
        @foreach (var item in Items)
        {
            @*The UI markup for the RowTemplate*@
            @*RenderFragment parameter will be*@
            @*applied here*@
            <tr>@RowTemplate(item)</tr>
        }
    </tbody>
    <tfoot>
        @*TableFooter will be inserted here*@
        <tr>@TableFooter</tr>
    </tfoot>
</table>
@code {
    [Parameter]
    public
        RenderFragment TableHeader
    { get; set; }
    [Parameter]
    public
        RenderFragment<TItem> RowTemplate
    { get; set; }
    [Parameter]
    public
        RenderFragment TableFooter
    { get; set; }
    // A collection of any type can be
    // passed for Items
    [Parameter]
    public
        IReadOnlyList<TItem> Items
    { get; set; }
}
```

To *consume* the template, add the following code to the **FetchData.razor** page:

```razor
<TableTemplate Items="forecasts" Context="forecast">
    <TableHeader>
        <th>Date of Forecast</th>
        <th>Summary</th>
        <th></th>
    </TableHeader>
    <RowTemplate>
        <td><b>@forecast.Date.Value.ToLongDateString()</b></td>
        <td>-- <i>@forecast.Summary</i> --</td>
        <td>
            <!-- Edit the current forecast -->
            <button class="btn btn-primary"
                    @onclick="(() => EditForecast(forecast))">
                Edit
            </button>
        </td>
    </RowTemplate>
</TableTemplate>
```

```
<TableTemplate Items="forecasts" Context="forecast">
    <TableHeader>
        <th>Date of Forecast</th>
        <th>Summary</th>
        <th></th>
    </TableHeader>
    <RowTemplate>
        <td><b>@forecast.Date.Value.ToLongDateString()</b></td>
        <td>-- <i>@forecast.Summary</i> --</td>
        <td>
            <!-- Edit the current forecast -->
            <button class="btn btn-primary"
                    @onclick="(() => EditForecast(forecast))">
                Edit
            </button>
        </td>
    </RowTemplate>
</TableTemplate>
```

```
@typeparam TItem

<table class="table">
    <thead>
        <tr>@TableHeader</tr>
    </thead>
    <tbody>
        @foreach (var item in Items)
        {
            <tr>@RowTemplate(item)</tr>
        }
    </tbody>
    <tfoot>
        <tr>@TableFooter</tr>
    </tfoot>
</table>
```

Essentially, we pass in a *collection* for **Items** and define a **custom UI** for the **@TableHeader** and **@RowTemplate** *RenderFragments* (in this example, we don't pass a value for the **@TableFooter** *RenderFragment* so it will remain blank).

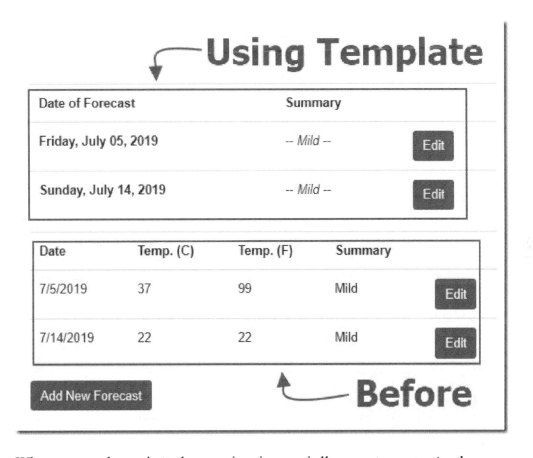

When we *run* the project, the *templated control* allows us to *customize* the instance of the control while retaining the structure and logic of the **HTML table**.

```
<TableTemplate Items="forecasts" Context="forecast">
    <TableHeader>
        <th>Date of Forecast</th>
        <th>Summary</th>
        <th></th>
    </TableHeader>
    <RowTemplate>
        <td><b>@forecast.Date.Value.ToLongDateString()</b></td>
        <td>-- <i>@forecast.Summary</i> --</td>
        <td>
            <!-- Edit the current forecast -->
            <button class="btn btn-primary"
                    @onclick="(() => EditForecast(forecast))">
                Edit
            </button>
        </td>
    </RowTemplate>
</TableTemplate>
```

Note: When you use the generic **RenderFragment\<T>** parameter in your **templated component**, the type that you pass as \<T> will have a variable name of *context* inside the **templated component.** However, you can override this by setting the *Context=* parameter.

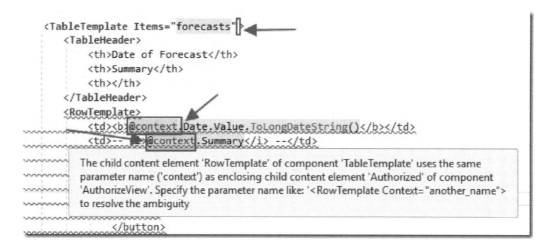

When you have other controls on the page that are already using the default *context* parameter, you will find that the page will not *build* and you will get an error like this:

> CS0136   A local or parameter named 'context' cannot be declared in this scope because that name is used in an enclosing local scope to define a local or parameter

or like this:

> The child content element 'RowTemplate' of component 'TableTemplate' uses the same parameter name ('context') as enclosing child content element 'Authorized' of component 'AuthorizeView'. Specify the parameter name like: '<RowTemplate Context="another_name"> to resolve the ambiguity

Chapter 8: Blazor JavaScript Interop

The sample code for this chapter can be obtained at the link "Blazor JavaScript Interop" at http://BlazorHelpWebsite.com/Downloads.aspx

When you need to, you can interact with **JavaScript** using **Blazor**. This allows you to call **Javascript** methods from **Blazor** and call **Blazor** methods from **JavaScript** as well as pass parameters.

Starting With State Manager

We will start with the project created in the chapter: **Implementing State Management In Blazor**.

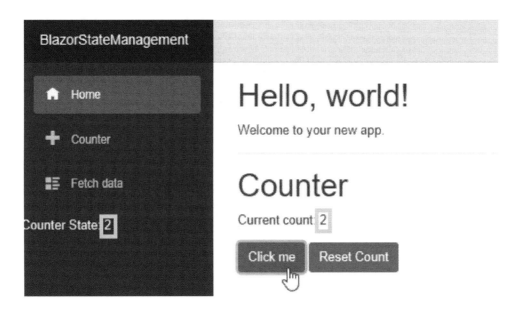

That project allows you to *persist data* between **Blazor** pages. In that example, the value for the **counter** is maintained.

However, when you *restart* the application, the **counter** starts over again.

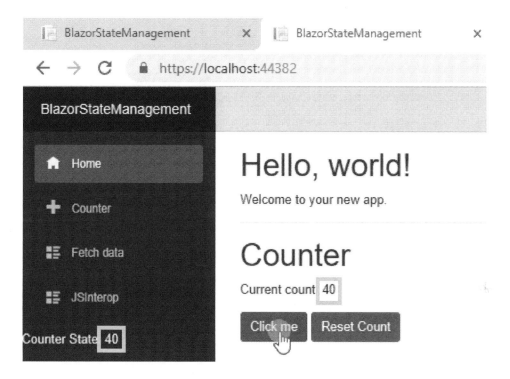

In this example, we will persist the **counter value** between *application restarts*, and even between **multiple tabs** in the same web browser.

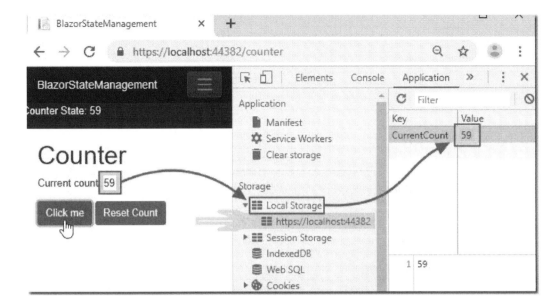

We will do this by storing the **counter** value in the user's web browser's **Local Storage**.

We communicate with **Local Storage** through **JavaScript**.

With **Blazor**, we communicate with **JavaScript** using **JavaScript Interop**.

Using JavaScript Interop

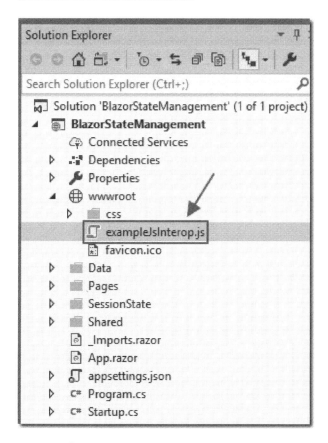

To demonstrate how **JavaScript Interop** in **Blazor** works, we will start with two simple examples.

Open the project created in the chapter **Implementing State Management in Blazor** in **Visual Studio** and add a **JavaScript** file called **exampleJsInterop.js** to the **wwwroot** directory using the following code:

```
(function () {
    window.exampleJsFunctions = {
        helloWorld: function () {
            return alert('Hello World!');
        }
    };
})();
```

This adds a **JavaScript** method called *helloWorld* that simply displays an **alert box**.

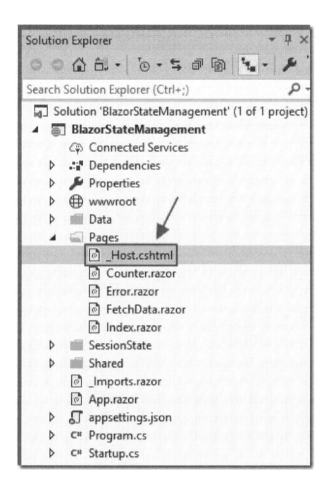

To allow this **JavaScript** to be called, it needs to be registered in the main HTML page.

Open the **_Host.cshtml** file, and add the following line below the `<script src="_framework/blazor.server.js"></script>` line:

```
<script src="exampleJsInterop.js"></script>
```

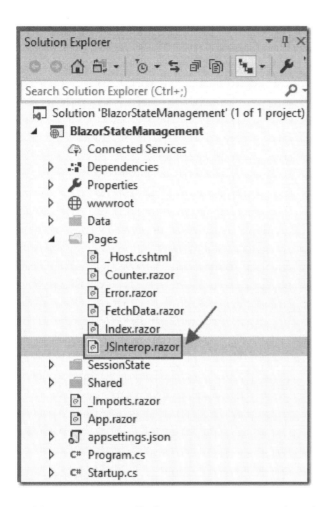

Add a new page called **JSInterop.razor** using the following code:

```
@page "/JSInterop"
@*Inject JSRuntime to allow JavaScript Interop *@
@inject IJSRuntime JSRuntime
<h1>JavaScript Interop</h1>
<div>
    <button type="button"
            class="btn btn-primary"
            @onclick="HelloWorld">
        Hello World
    </button>
</div>
@code {
    public async void HelloWorld()
    {
        // helloWorld is implemented in
        // wwwroot /exampleJsInterop.js
        await JSRuntime.InvokeAsync<string>(
            "exampleJsFunctions.helloWorld", null
            );
    }
}
```

Essentially, we inject support for **JavaScript Interop** by adding the line:

```
@inject IJSRuntime JSRuntime
```

We then call the *helloWorld* **JavaScript** method, created earlier, using **JSRuntime.InvokeAsync** like so:

247

```
await JSRuntime.InvokeAsync<string>(
    "exampleJsFunctions.helloWorld", null
    );
```

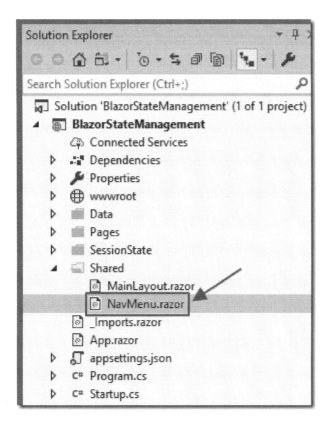

Now, open **NavMenu.razor** and *add* the following code so that a *link* to the new page shows up in the **menu**:

```
<li class="nav-item px-3">
    <NavLink class="nav-link" href="JSInterop">
        <span class="oi oi-list-rich" aria-hidden="true"></span> JSInterop
    </NavLink>
</li>
```

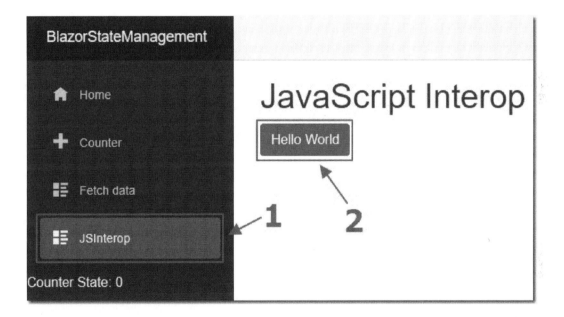

When we *run* the application, we can *navigate* to the **JSInterop** page and *click* the **Hello World** button.

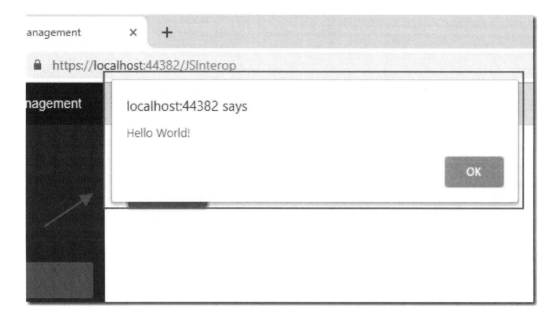

A **JavaScript** alert box will appear.

From JavaScript Back to Blazor with Parameters

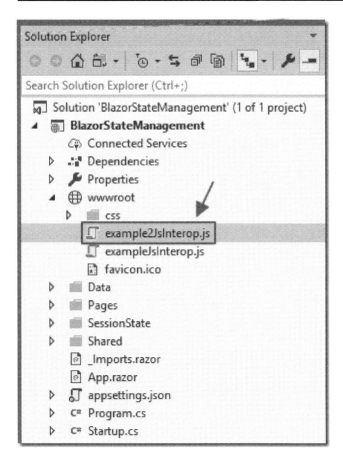

To demonstrate how a **JavaScript** function can take *parameters* and communicate back to **Blazor**, add a new **JavaScript** file to the **wwwroot** directory, **example2JsInterop.js**, using the following code:

```
(function () {
    window.example2JsFunctions = {
        showPrompt: function (text) {
            return prompt(text, 'Type your name here');
        }
    };
})();
```

To register the **JavaScript** file, add the following line to the **_Host.cshtml** page:

```
<script src="example2JsInterop.js"></script>
```

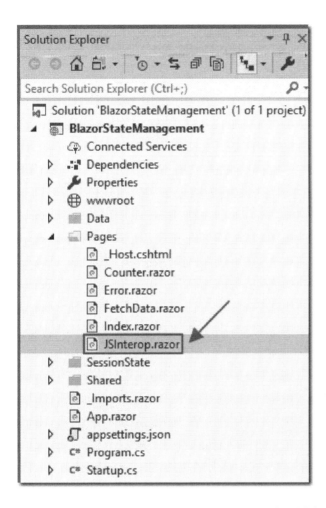

Next, open the **JSInterop.razor** page and *add* the following **HTML markup**:

```
<br />
<div>
    <button type="button"
            class="btn btn-primary"
            @onclick="SayMyName">
        Say My Name
    </button>
    <br />
    <p>@strSayMyName</p>
</div>
```

Finally, add the following code to implement the **SayMyName** method:

```
string strSayMyName = "";
 public async void SayMyName()
 {
     // showPrompt is implemented in wwwroot/example2JsInterop.js
     var NameFromJavaScript =
         await JSRuntime.InvokeAsync<string>(
             "example2JsFunctions.showPrompt",
             "What's your name?"
             );
     strSayMyName = $"Your name is: {NameFromJavaScript}";
     // Must call StateHasChanged() because Blazor
     // will not know to refresh page because
     // it was updated by JavaScript
     StateHasChanged();
 }
```

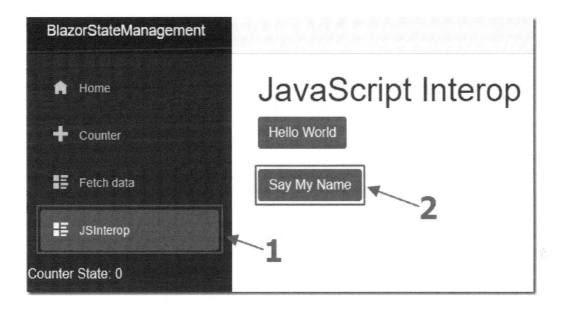

When we *run* the application, we can *navigate* to the **JSInterop** page, and *click* the **Say My Name** button.

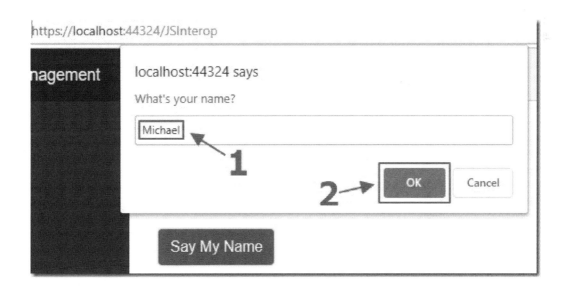

We enter our **name** in the **JavaScript** *dialog box* and click **OK**.

The **Blazor** page then displays a message with our **name**.

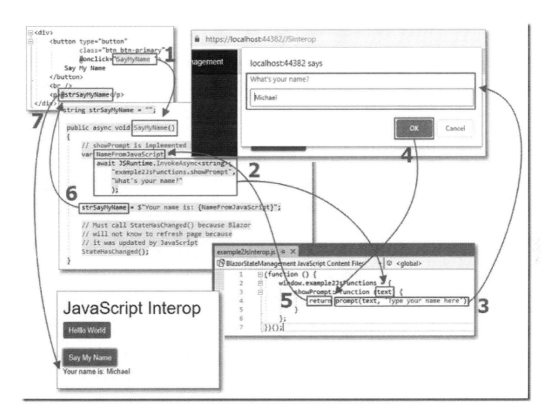

The image above illustrates the program flow.

Using ElementReference and the @ref Attribute

⚓ **Go Make Things**

About   Daily Tips   Learn JS

December 31, 2014

Getting HTML asynchronously from another page (with native JavaScript)

On a recent project, I needed to load the form on a contact page in a modal window on a different page.

That's typically something you'd turn to jQuery for, but I want to show you can achieve the same effect with native JavaScript.

Let's say we want to fill a **Popup** with content from another page.

We can use **JavaScript** from the article: **Getting HTML asynchronously from another page (with native JavaScript)** (https://gomakethings.com/getting-html-asynchronously-from-another-page/).

We now need to call this **JavaScript**, pass it the web address of the page we want to *retrieve*, get the *results* of the call, and *insert* the **contents returned** into our **Popup**.

However, to get the **HTML contents** of the page retrieved with the **JavaScript** call onto the page in the **Blazor** application, we need to use the **ElementReference** and the **@ref** attribute.

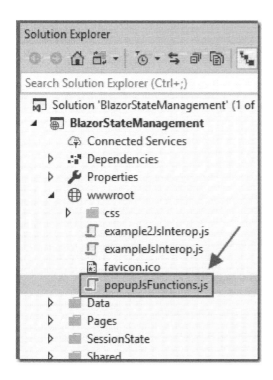

The first step is to create a new **JavaScript** file called **popupJsFunctions.js** and add the following code:

```javascript
(function () {
    window.popupJsFunctions = {
        populateDiv: function (element) {
            popupJsFunctions.getHTML('/Counter',
                function (response) {
                element.innerHTML = response.documentElement.innerHTML;
            });
        },
        // From:
        // https://gomakethings.com/getting-html-asynchronously-from-another-page/
        getHTML: function (url, callback) {
            // Feature detection
            if (!window.XMLHttpRequest) return;
            // Create new request
            var xhr = new XMLHttpRequest();
            // Setup callback
            xhr.onload = function () {
                if (callback && typeof (callback) === 'function') {
                    callback(this.responseXML);
                }
            };
            // Get the HTML
            xhr.open('GET', url);
            xhr.responseType = 'document';
            xhr.send();
        }
    };
})();
```

This step simply creates a **JavaScript** method called **getHTML** that will retrieve the contents of an HTML page.

This step also adds a **JavaScript** method, called **populateDiv**, which when passed a **ElementReference**, will populate it with the contents returned by the **getHTML JavaScript** method.

Ensure that we register the **JavaScript** file in the **_Host.cshtml** page by adding this line:

```
<script src="popupJsFunctions.js"></script>
```

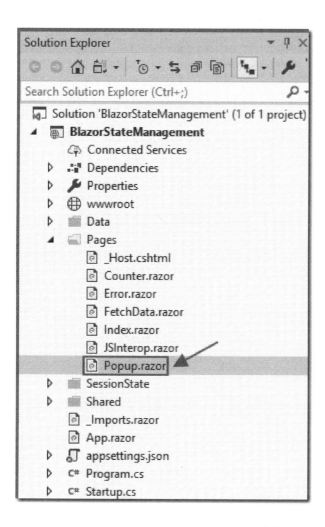

Next, add a new page, **Popup.razor**, using the following code:

```
@page "/Popup"
@inject IJSRuntime JSRuntime
<h1>Popup</h1>
<button class="btn btn-primary"
        @onclick="ShowDynamicPopup">
    Show Dynamic Popup
</button>
@if (showDynamicPopup)
{
    <div tabindex="-1" style="display:block" role="dialog">
        <div class="modal-dialog">
            <div class="modal-content">
                <div class="modal-header">
                    <h3 class="modal-title">Blazor Dynamic Popup</h3>
                    <button type="button"
                            class="close"
                            @onclick="HideDynamicPopup">
                        <span aria-hidden="true">X</span>
                    </button>
                </div>
                <div @ref="modalBody"
                     class="modal-body">
                    <!-- Dynamic content will go here -->
                </div>
            </div>
        </div>
    </div>
}
```

```
@code {
    ElementReference modalBody; // reference to the DIV
    bool showDynamicPopup = false;
    // To prevent making JavaScript interop calls during prerendering
    protected override async Task OnAfterRenderAsync(bool firstRender)
    {
        // This will set the content of the Div
        // to the content of the server Login page
        await setDivContent(modalBody);
    }
    public async Task setDivContent(ElementReference elementRef)
    {
        // Call the popupJsFunctions.populateDiv
        // JavaScript method, passing it an instance of
        // the DIV element from the page (elementRef)
        // This DIV will be populated with the HTML content
        // Of the page retrieved
        await JSRuntime.InvokeAsync<object>(
            "popupJsFunctions.populateDiv", elementRef
            );
    }
    void ShowDynamicPopup()
    {
        showDynamicPopup = true;
    }
    void HideDynamicPopup()
    {
        showDynamicPopup = false;
    }
}
```

Note that <!-- Dynamic content will go here - -> is contained in a **Div**.

The key thing here is that we added "**ref=modalBody**" to the **Div**.

263

```
<div tabindex="-1" style="display:block" role="dialog">
    <div class="modal-dialog">
        <div class="modal-content">
            <div class="modal-header">
                <h3 class="modal-title">Blazor Dynamic Popup</h3>
                <button type="button"
                        class="close"
                        @onclick="HideDynamicPopup">
                    <span aria-hidden="true">X</span>
                </button>
            </div>
            <div @ref="modalBody"
                 class="modal-body">
                <!-- Dynamic content will go here -->
            </div>
        </div>
    </div>
</div>
}
@code {
    ElementReference modalBody; // reference to the DIV
    bool showDynamicPopup = false;
    // To prevent making JavaScript interop calls during prerendering
    protected override async Task OnAfterRenderAsync(bool firstRender)
    {
        // This will set the content of the Div
        // to the content of the server Login page
        await setDivContent(modalBody);
    }
    public async Task setDivContent(ElementReference elementRef)
    {
        // Call the popupJsFunctions.populateDiv
        // JavaScript method, passing it an instance of
        // the DIV element from the page (elementRef)
        // This DIV will be populated with the HTML content
        // Of the page retrieved
        await JSRuntime.InvokeAsync<object>(
            "popupJsFunctions.populateDiv", elementRef
            );
    }
```

This allows us to access the **Div** (as an **ElementReference**) in the **setDivContent** method and *pass* it as a parameter to the ***populateDiv*** JavaScript function.

Now, open **NavMenu.razor** and *add* the following code so that a *link* to the new page shows up in the **menu**:

```
<li class="nav-item px-3">
    <NavLink class="nav-link" href="Popup">
        <span class="oi oi-list-rich" aria-hidden="true"></span> Popup
    </NavLink>
</li>
```

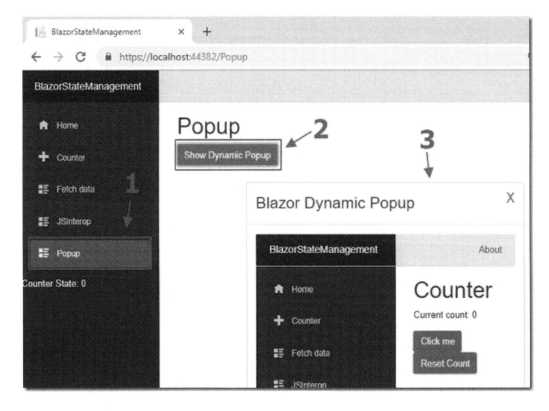

When we run the application, we can now click the **Show Dynamic Popup** button to display the **Popup** with the dynamically retrieved content.

(**Note:** Only the *html content* is retrieved, not its associated **JavaScript**, so the page inside the popup won't work.)

Blazor State Management Using Local Storage

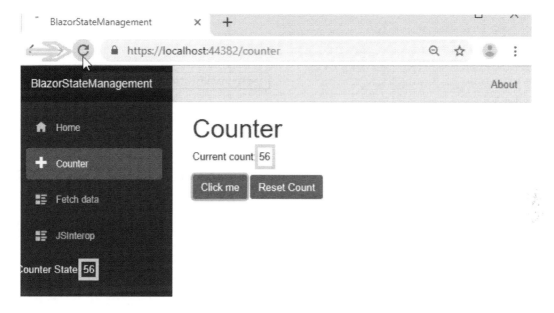

In the final example, we will demonstrate *refactoring* the existing **State Management** to use the web browser **Local Storage**.

This will allow the value of the **counter** to be persisted when the user *closes* and *re-opens* their **web browser**.

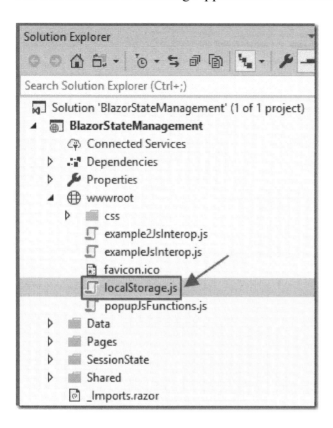

First, add a new file, **localStorage.js** to the **wwwroot folder** using the following code from: **https://github.com/dotnet-presentations/blazor-workshop**:

```
// From: https://github.com/dotnet-presentations/blazor-workshop
// (c) Microsoft
(function () {
    window.blazorLocalStorage = {
        get: key => key in localStorage ? JSON.parse(localStorage[key]) : null,
        set: (key, value) => { localStorage[key] = JSON.stringify(value); },
        delete: key => { delete localStorage[key]; }
    };
})();
```

Ensure that we register the **JavaScript** file in the **_Host.cshtml** page by adding this line:

```
<script src="localStorage.js"></script>
```

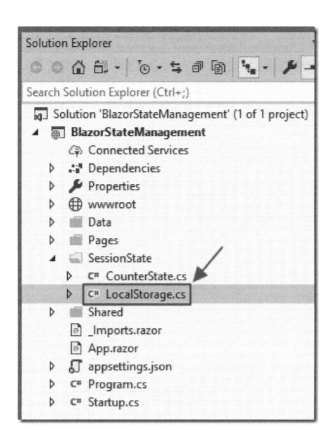

Create a new **class file** called **LocalStorage.cs** using the following code from:

https://github.com/dotnet-presentations/blazor-workshop:

```csharp
using Microsoft.JSInterop;
using System.Threading.Tasks;
// From https://github.com/dotnet-presentations/blazor-workshop
// (c) Microsoft
namespace BlazingPizza.ComponentsLibrary
{
    public static class LocalStorage
    {
        public static ValueTask<T> GetAsync<T>
            (IJSRuntime jsRuntime, string key)
            => jsRuntime.InvokeAsync<T>(
                "blazorLocalStorage.get", key
                );
        public static ValueTask<T> SetAsync<T>
            (IJSRuntime jsRuntime, string key, object value)
            => jsRuntime.InvokeAsync<T>(
                "blazorLocalStorage.set", key, value
                );
        public static ValueTask<T> DeleteAsync<T>
            (IJSRuntime jsRuntime, string key)
            => jsRuntime.InvokeAsync<T>(
                "blazorLocalStorage.delete", key
                );
    }
}
```

This time we are creating a *helper class* to call the **JavaScript** function.

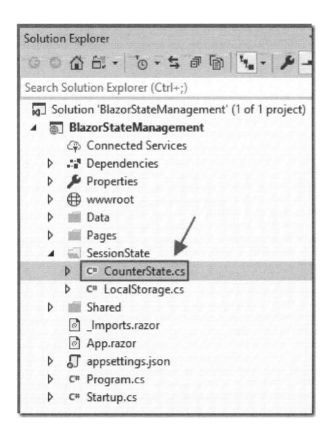

Next, open the existing **CounterState.cs** class and *replace all the code* with the following:

```csharp
using System;
using System.Collections.Generic;
using System.Linq;
using System.Threading.Tasks;
using Microsoft.JSInterop;
using BlazingPizza.ComponentsLibrary;
namespace BlazorStateManagement
{
    public class CounterState
    {
        // A property to hod reference to JSRuntime
        private readonly IJSRuntime _jsRuntime;
        private int? _currentCount = 0;
        // To use JSRuntime in a class, we must
        // inject it into the constructor of the class
        // using dependency injection
        public CounterState(IJSRuntime jsRuntime)
        {
            _jsRuntime = jsRuntime;
        }
        // StateChanged is an event handler other pages
        // can subscribe to
        public event EventHandler StateChanged;
        public int CurrentCount()
        {
            return (!_currentCount.HasValue) ? 0 : (int)_currentCount.Value;
        }
        public async Task<int> GetCurrentCount()
        {
            try
            {
                // We call LocalStorage to get the current count
                _currentCount =
                    await LocalStorage.GetAsync<int>(_jsRuntime, "CurrentCount");
            }
            catch
            {
                // we did not have a value in LocalStorage
                // Set it
                _currentCount = 0;
                SetCurrentCount(_currentCount.Value);
            }
            return (!_currentCount.HasValue) ? 0 : (int)_currentCount.Value;
        }
```

272

```csharp
        // This method will be called to update the current count
        public async void SetCurrentCount(int paramCount)
        {
            // We use LocalStorage to set the current count
            await
                LocalStorage.SetAsync<object>(_jsRuntime, "CurrentCount", paramCount);
            _currentCount = paramCount;
            StateHasChanged();
        }
        // This method will allow us to reset the current count
        public void ResetCurrentCount()
        {
            // We use LocalStorage to clear the current count
            LocalStorage.SetAsync<object>(_jsRuntime, "CurrentCount", 0);
            _currentCount = 0;
            StateHasChanged();
        }
        private void StateHasChanged()
        {
            // This will update any subscribers
            // that the counter state has changed
            // so they can update themseleves
            // and show the current counter value
            StateChanged?.Invoke(this, EventArgs.Empty);
        }
    }
}
```

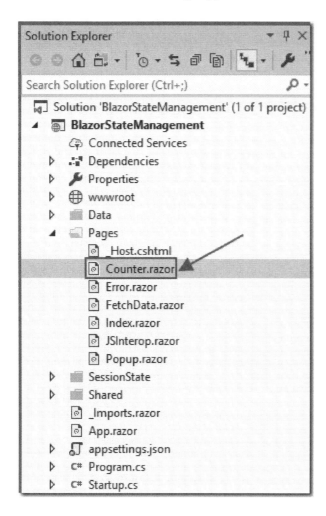

The **GetCurrentCount** method now returns a *Task,* so we have to refactor the code that calls it.

Open the **Counter.razor** page and replace *all the code* with the following:

```
@page "/counter"
@inject CounterState CounterState
<h1>Counter</h1>
<!-- We now call the GetCurrentCount() method -->
<!-- to get the current count -->
<p>Current count: @CurrentCount</p>
<button class="btn btn-primary"
        @onclick="IncrementCount">
    Click me
</button>
<!-- Add a button to reset the current count -->
<!-- that calls the CounterState class directly -->
<button class="btn btn-primary"
        @onclick="CounterState.ResetCurrentCount">
    Reset Count
</button>
@code {
    int CurrentCount;
    // To prevent making JavaScript interop calls during prerendering
    protected override async Task OnAfterRenderAsync(bool firstRender)
    {
        CurrentCount = await CounterState.GetCurrentCount();
        StateHasChanged();
    }
    async void IncrementCount()
    {
        // Call the GetCurrentCount() method
        // to get the current count
        int CurrentCount = await CounterState.GetCurrentCount();
        // Increase the count
        CurrentCount++;
        // Set Current count on the Session State object
        CounterState.SetCurrentCount(CurrentCount);
    }
}
```

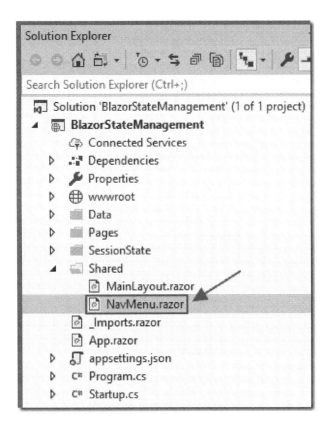

We also need to open **NavMenu.razor** and replace the following code:

```
<div>
    <!-- We now call the GetCurrentCount() method -->
    <!-- to get the current count -->
    <p style="color:white">
        Counter State: @CounterState.GetCurrentCount()
    </p>
</div>
```

with:

```
<div>
    <!-- We now call the CurrentCount() method -->
    <!-- to get the current count -->
    <p style="color:white">
        Counter State: @CounterState.CurrentCount()
    </p>
</div>
```

In the @code section, add the following code to retrieve the current counter value:

```
// To prevent making JavaScript interop calls during prerendering
protected override async Task OnAfterRenderAsync(bool firstRender)
{
    // We only want this to run one time
    if (firstRender)
    {
        await CounterState.GetCurrentCount();
        // Must call StateHasChanged() because Blazor
        // will not know to refresh page because
        // it was updated by JavaScript
        StateHasChanged();
    }
}
```

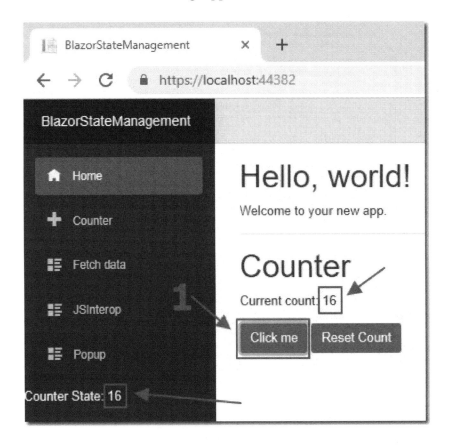

Now, when we *run* the application, the **counter value** will *persist*.

Chapter 9: A Demonstration of Simple Server-Side Blazor Cookie Authentication

The sample code for this chapter can be obtained at the link "A Demonstration of Simple Server-Side Blazor Cookie Authentication" at http://BlazorHelpWebsite.com/Downloads.aspx

To demonstrate how **authentication** works in a server-side **Blazor** application, we will strip **authentication** down to its most basic elements. We will simply *set* a **cookie** then *read* that **cookie** in the application.

Application Authentication

Most business web applications require their users to **log into** the application.

The user enters their **username** and **password**, which are checked against a *membership database*.

Once *authenticated*, the application recognizes the **user**, and the application now has the ability to deliver content *securely*.

Once the *authentication process* of a server-side **Blazor** application is understood, we can then implement an **authentication** and **membership management** system that meets our needs (for example, one that allows users to create and manage their user accounts).

NOTE: This sample code **does not check to see if a person is using a legitimate username and password!** You would need to add the proper code to check the username and password. This code is just a demonstration of how the process of *authorizing* a user works.

Create the Application

Open **Visual Studio 2019**.

Create a new Blazor app

Create a **Blazor Server App** <u>without</u> authentication.

Add Nuget Packages

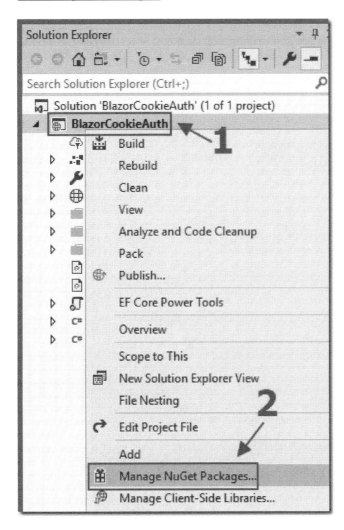

In the **Solution Explorer**, *right-click* on the *client* project and select **Manage NuGet Packages**.

Add references to the following libraries:

- Microsoft.AspNetCore.Authorization
- Microsoft.AspNetCore.Http
- Microsoft.AspNetCore.Blazor.HttpClient
- Microsoft.AspNetCore.Identity

Add Cookie Authentication

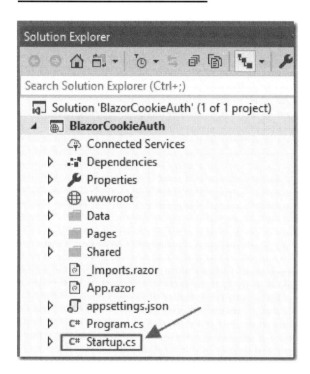

Open the **Startup.cs** file.

Add the following *using statements* to the top of the file:

```
// ******
// BLAZOR COOKIE Auth Code (begin)
using Microsoft.AspNetCore.Authentication.Cookies;
using Microsoft.AspNetCore.Http;
using System.Net.Http;
// BLAZOR COOKIE Auth Code (end)
// ******
```

Alter the **Startup** class to the following, adding the sections marked **BLAZOR COOKIE Auth Code**:

```
public class Startup
{
    public Startup(IConfiguration configuration)
    {
        Configuration = configuration;
    }
    public IConfiguration Configuration { get; }
    public void ConfigureServices(IServiceCollection services)
    {
        // ******
        // BLAZOR COOKIE Auth Code (begin)
        services.Configure<CookiePolicyOptions>(options =>
        {
            options.CheckConsentNeeded = context => true;
            options.MinimumSameSitePolicy = SameSiteMode.None;
        });
        services.AddAuthentication(
            CookieAuthenticationDefaults.AuthenticationScheme)
            .AddCookie();
        // BLAZOR COOKIE Auth Code (end)
        // ******
        services.AddRazorPages();
        services.AddServerSideBlazor();
        services.AddSingleton<WeatherForecastService>();
        // ******
        // BLAZOR COOKIE Auth Code (begin)
        // From: https://github.com/aspnet/Blazor/issues/1554
        // HttpContextAccessor
        services.AddHttpContextAccessor();
        services.AddScoped<HttpContextAccessor>();
        services.AddHttpClient();
        services.AddScoped<HttpClient>();
        // BLAZOR COOKIE Auth Code (end)
        // ******
    }
```

```
// This method gets called by the runtime.
// Use this method to configure the HTTP request pipeline.
public void Configure(IApplicationBuilder app, IWebHostEnvironment env)
{
    if (env.IsDevelopment())
    {
        app.UseDeveloperExceptionPage();
    }
    else
    {
        app.UseExceptionHandler("/Home/Error");
        app.UseHsts();
    }
    app.UseHttpsRedirection();
    app.UseStaticFiles();
    app.UseRouting();
    // ******
    // BLAZOR COOKIE Auth Code (begin)
    app.UseHttpsRedirection();
    app.UseStaticFiles();
    app.UseCookiePolicy();
    app.UseAuthentication();
    // BLAZOR COOKIE Auth Code (end)
    // ******
    app.UseEndpoints(endpoints =>
    {
        endpoints.MapBlazorHub();
        endpoints.MapFallbackToPage("/_Host");
    });
}
```

First, the code adds support for *cookies*. Cookies are created by the application, and passed to the user's web browser when the user logs in. The web browser passes the cookie back to the application to indicate that the user is *authenticated*. When the user 'logs out,' the cookie is removed.

This code also adds:

- HttpContextAccessor
- HttpClient

as *services* that will be accessed in the code using *dependency Injection*.

Add Login/Logout Pages

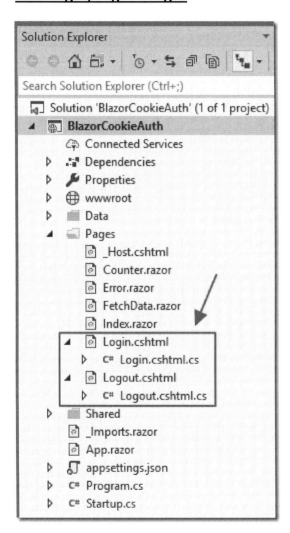

Logging in (and out) is performed by **.cshtml** pages.

Add the following **Razor pages** and code:

Login.cshtml

```
@page
@model BlazorCookieAuth.Server.Pages.LoginModel
@{
    ViewData["Title"] = "Log in";
}
<h2>Login</h2>
```

Login.cshtml.cs

```
using System;
using System.Collections.Generic;
using System.Security.Claims;
using System.Threading.Tasks;
using Microsoft.AspNetCore.Authentication;
using Microsoft.AspNetCore.Authentication.Cookies;
using Microsoft.AspNetCore.Authorization;
using Microsoft.AspNetCore.Mvc;
using Microsoft.AspNetCore.Mvc.RazorPages;
namespace BlazorCookieAuth.Server.Pages
{
    [AllowAnonymous]
    public class LoginModel : PageModel
    {
        public string ReturnUrl { get; set; }
        public async Task<IActionResult>
            OnGetAsync(string paramUsername, string paramPassword)
        {
            string returnUrl = Url.Content("~/");
            try
            {
                // Clear the existing external cookie
                await HttpContext
                    .SignOutAsync(
                    CookieAuthenticationDefaults.AuthenticationScheme);
            }
            catch { }
            // *** !!! This is where you would validate the user !!! ***
            // In this example we just log the user in
            // (Always log the user in for this demo)
            var claims = new List<Claim>
            {
                new Claim(ClaimTypes.Name, paramUsername),
                new Claim(ClaimTypes.Role, "Administrator"),
            };
            var claimsIdentity = new ClaimsIdentity(
                claims, CookieAuthenticationDefaults.AuthenticationScheme);
            var authProperties = new AuthenticationProperties
            {
                IsPersistent = true,
                RedirectUri = this.Request.Host.Value
            };
            try
            {
                await HttpContext.SignInAsync(
                CookieAuthenticationDefaults.AuthenticationScheme,
                new ClaimsPrincipal(claimsIdentity),
                authProperties);
            }
            catch (Exception ex)
            {
                string error = ex.Message;
            }
            return LocalRedirect(returnUrl);
        }
    }
}
```

Logout.cshtml

```
@page
@model BlazorCookieAuth.Server.Pages.LogoutModel
@{
    ViewData["Title"] = "Logout";
}
<h2>Logout</h2>
```

Logout.cshtml.cs

```
using System;
using System.Threading.Tasks;
using Microsoft.AspNetCore.Authentication;
using Microsoft.AspNetCore.Authentication.Cookies;
using Microsoft.AspNetCore.Mvc;
using Microsoft.AspNetCore.Mvc.RazorPages;
namespace BlazorCookieAuth.Server.Pages
{
    public class LogoutModel : PageModel
    {
        public async Task<IActionResult> OnGetAsync()
        {
            // Clear the existing external cookie
            await HttpContext
                .SignOutAsync(
                CookieAuthenticationDefaults.AuthenticationScheme);
            return LocalRedirect(Url.Content("~/"));
        }
    }
}
```

Add Client Code

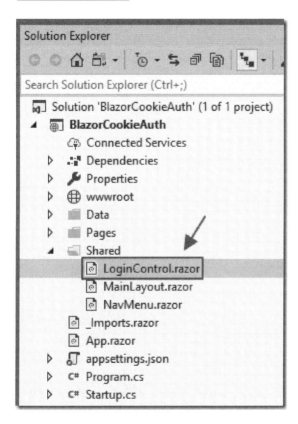

Add a page called **LoginControl.razor** to the **Shared** folder using the following code:

```
@page "/loginControl"
<AuthorizeView>
    <Authorized>
        <b>Hello, @context.User.Identity.Name!</b>
        <a class="ml-md-auto btn btn-primary"
           href="/logout?returnUrl=/"
           target="_top">Logout</a>
    </Authorized>
    <NotAuthorized>
        <input type="text"
               placeholder="User Name"
               @bind="@Username" />
          
        <input type="password"
               placeholder="Password"
               @bind="@Password" />
        <a class="ml-md-auto btn btn-primary"
           href="/login?paramUsername=@Username&paramPassword=@Password"
           target="_top">Login</a>
    </NotAuthorized>
</AuthorizeView>
@code {
    string Username = "";
    string Password = "";
}
```

This code creates a *login component* that uses the **AuthorizeView** component to wrap markup code based on the **user's** current *authentication*.

If the **user** is *logged in*, we display their name and a **Logout** button (that navigates the user to the *logout page* created earlier).

If they are not *logged in*, we display **username** and **password** boxes and a **Login** button (that navigates the user to the *login page* created earlier).

294

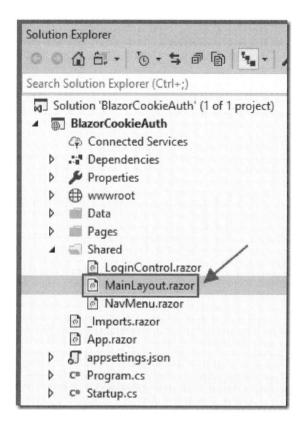

Finally, we alter the **MainLayout.razor** page (in the **Shared** folder) to the following:

```
@inherits LayoutComponentBase
<div class="sidebar">
    <NavMenu />
</div>
<div class="main">
    <div class="top-row px-4">
        <!-- BLAZOR COOKIE Auth Code (begin) -->
        <LoginControl />
        <!-- BLAZOR COOKIE Auth Code (end) -->
    </div>
    <div class="content px-4">
        @Body
    </div>
</div>
```

This adds the *login component* to the top of every page in the **Blazor** application.

```
App.razor  ⊹ ×
    1    <CascadingAuthenticationState>
    2        <Router AppAssembly="@typeof(Program).Assembly">
    3            <Found Context="routeData">
    4                <RouteView RouteData="@routeData" DefaultLayout="@typeof(MainLayout)" />
    5            </Found>
    6            <NotFound>
    7                <LayoutView Layout="@typeof(MainLayout)">
    8                    <p>Sorry, there's nothing at this address.</p>
    9                </LayoutView>
    10           </NotFound>
    11       </Router>
    12   </CascadingAuthenticationState>
```

Open the **App.razor** page and surround all the existing code in a **CascadingAuthenticationState** tag.

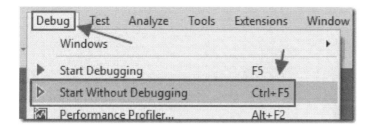

We can now hit **F5** to run the application.

We can enter a **username** and **password** and click the **Login** button…

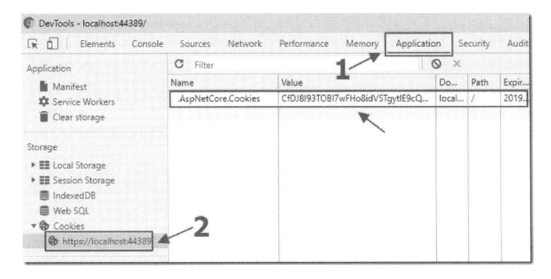

We can then look in the **Google Chrome Web Browser DevTools** and see the *cookie* has been created.

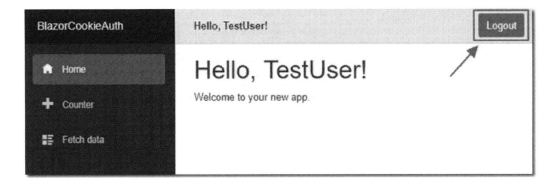

When we click **Logout**...

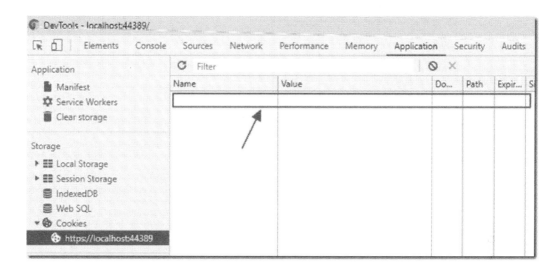

The *cookie* is removed.

Calling Server Side Controller Methods

At this point all the **.razor** pages will properly detect if the user is *authenticated* and operate as expected. However, if we make a *http request* to a **server side controller**, the **authenticated user** will <u>not be </u>properly detected.

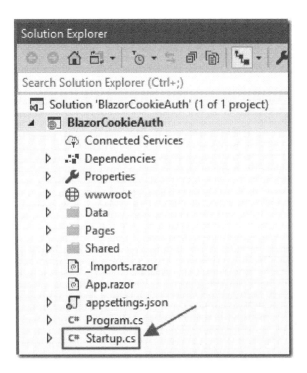

To demonstrate this, we first open the **startup.cs** page and add the following code to the end of the **app.UseEndpoints** method (under the **endpoints.MapFallbackToPage("/_Host");** line), to allow *http requests* to **controllers** to be *properly routed*:

```
// ******
// BLAZOR COOKIE Auth Code (begin)
endpoints.MapControllerRoute("default", "{controller=Home}/{action=Index}/{id?}");
// BLAZOR COOKIE Auth Code (end)
// ******
```

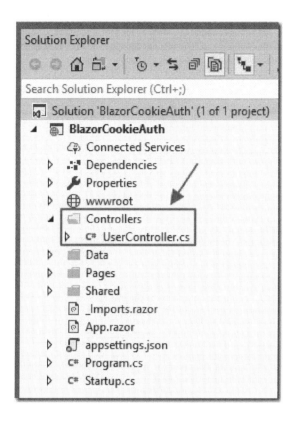

Next, we create a **Controllers** folder and add a **UserController.cs** file with the following code:

```
using Microsoft.AspNetCore.Mvc;
namespace BlazorCookieAuth.Controllers
{
    [Route("api/[controller]")]
    [ApiController]
    public class UserController : Controller
    {
        // /api/User/GetUser
        [HttpGet("[action]")]
        public UserModel GetUser()
        {
            // Instantiate a UserModel
            var userModel = new UserModel
            {
                UserName = "[]",
                IsAuthenticated = false
            };
            // Detect if the user is authenticated
            if (User.Identity.IsAuthenticated)
            {
                // Set the username of the authenticated user
                userModel.UserName =
                    User.Identity.Name;
                userModel.IsAuthenticated =
                    User.Identity.IsAuthenticated;
            };
            return userModel;
        }
    }
    // Class to hold the UserModel
    public class UserModel
    {
        public string UserName { get; set; }
        public bool IsAuthenticated { get; set; }
    }
}
```

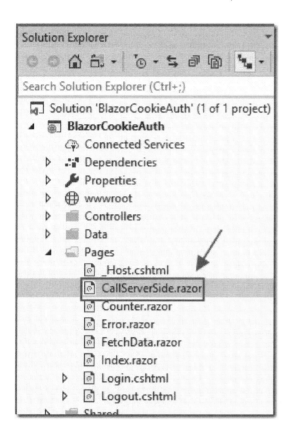

We add a new **.razor** page, **CallServerSide.razor**, using the following code:

```
@page "/CallServerSide"
@using BlazorCookieAuth.Controllers
@using System.Net.Http
@inject HttpClient Http
@inject NavigationManager UriHelper
@inject Microsoft.AspNetCore.Http.IHttpContextAccessor HttpContextAccessor
<h3>Call Server Side</h3>
<p>Current User: @CurrentUser.UserName</p>
<p>IsAuthenticated: @CurrentUser.IsAuthenticated</p>
<button class="btn btn-primary" @onclick="GetUser">Get User</button>
@code {
    UserModel CurrentUser = new UserModel();
    async Task GetUser()
    {
        // Call the server side controller
        var url = UriHelper.ToAbsoluteUri("/api/User/GetUser");
        var result = await Http.GetJsonAsync<UserModel>(url.ToString());
        // Update the result
        CurrentUser.UserName = result.UserName;
        CurrentUser.IsAuthenticated = result.IsAuthenticated;
    }
}
```

Finally, we use the following code to add a *link* to the page in
Shared/NavMenu.razor:

```
<li class="nav-item px-3">
    <NavLink class="nav-link" href="CallServerSide">
        <span class="oi oi-list-rich" aria-hidden="true"></span> Call Server Side
    </NavLink>
</li>
```

We *run* the application and **log in**.

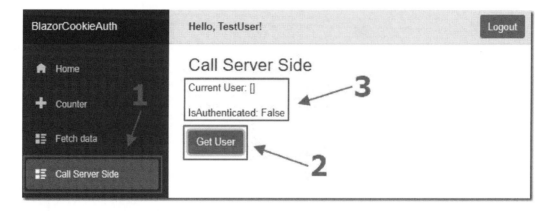

We *navigate* to the new **Call Server Side** control and click the **Get User** button (that calls the **UserController.cs** that we just added), and it <u>does not</u> detect the **logged in user**.

To resolve this, *change* the **GetUser** method in the **CallServerSide.razor** page to the following:

```
async Task GetUser()
{
    // Code courtesy from Oqtane.org (@sbwalker)
    // We must pass the authentication cookie in server side requests
    var authToken =
    HttpContextAccessor.HttpContext.Request.Cookies[".AspNetCore.Cookies"];
    if (authToken != null)
    {
        Http.DefaultRequestHeaders
        .Add("Cookie", ".AspNetCore.Cookies=" + authToken);
        // Call the server side controller
        var url = UriHelper.ToAbsoluteUri("/api/User/GetUser");
        var result = await Http.GetJsonAsync<UserModel>(url.ToString());
        // Update the result
        CurrentUser.UserName = result.UserName;
        CurrentUser.IsAuthenticated = result.IsAuthenticated;
    }
}
```

We have an *authentication cookie*; we just need to pass it in the
DefaultRequestHeaders.

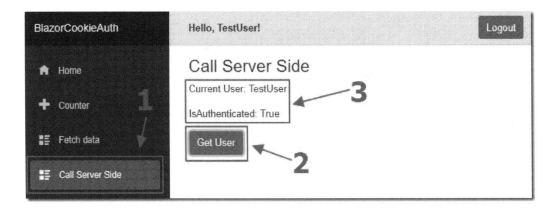

Now, when we **log in** and click the **Get User** button, the **controller** method is able to detect the **logged in user**.

Chapter 10: Deploying a Server Side Blazor Application To Azure

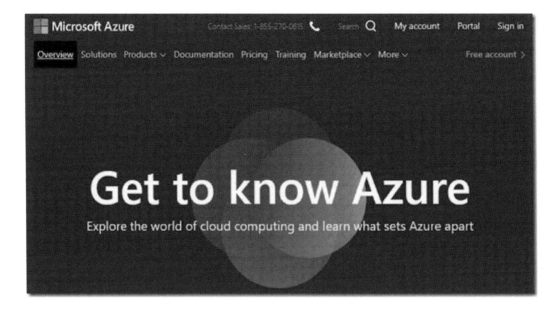

Microsoft Azure is a cloud service provider that allows you to *deploy* your **Blazor** application to be used by anyone in the world.

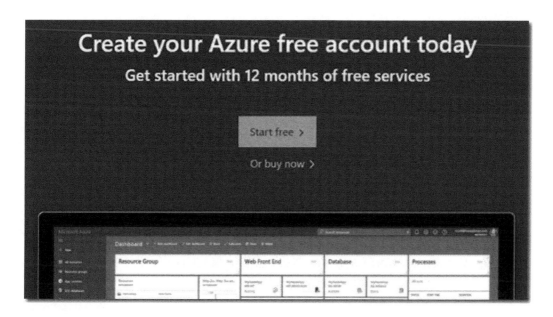

If you don't have a **Microsoft Azure** account, you can sign up for one here:

https://azure.microsoft.com/en-us/free

Create the Blazor Application

Open **Visual Studio**.

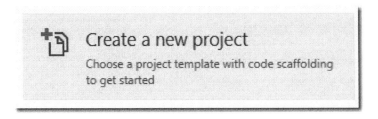

Select **Create a new Project**.

Select **Blazor App** and click **Next**.

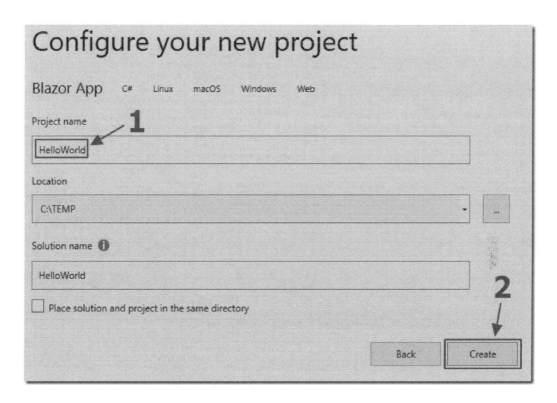

Give it a name and click **Create**.

Create a new Blazor app

Select **Blazor Server App** and click **Create**.

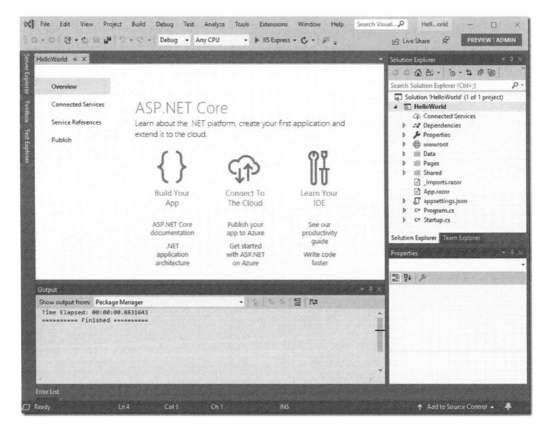

The application will open in **Visual Studio**.

Publish to Azure

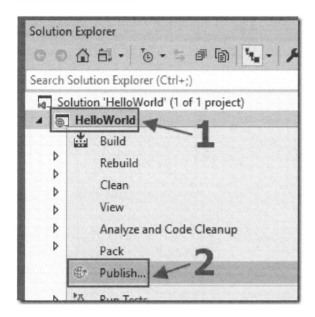

Right-click on the **project node** and select **Publish**.

When the **publishing wizard** comes up, select **Advanced**.

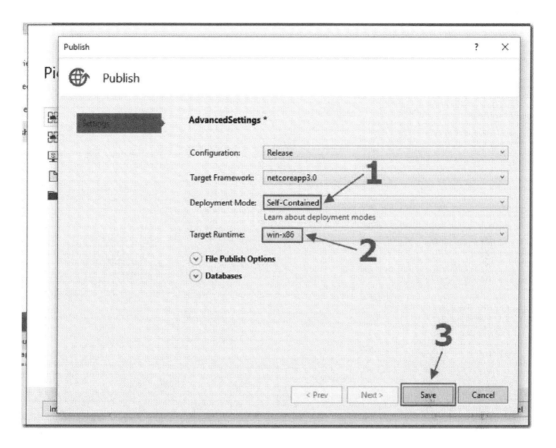

Select *Self-Contained* for **Deployment Mode** and *win-x86* for **Target Runtime** and click **Save**.

(**Note:** Once **.Net Core 3.0** is enabled on **Azure**, this step will no longer be required. The site: https://aspnetcoreon.azurewebsites.net/ will allow you to see when **.Net Core 3.0** is available in your **Azure** deployment location.)

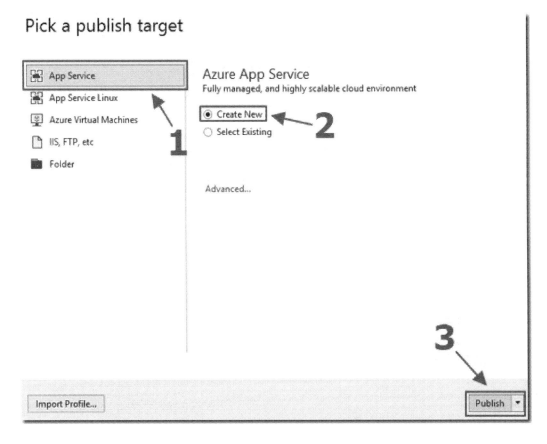

Back on the *publishing wizard*, select **App Service**, **Create New**, and click the **Publish** button.

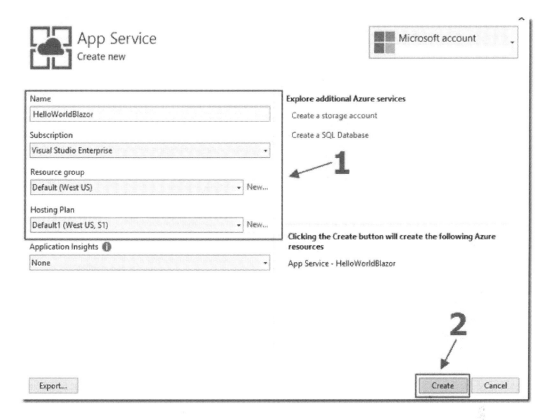

Fill out the information for your **App Service**, and click **Create**.

Note: If you need assistance with the settings see: ***Publish a Web app to Azure App Service using Visual Studio*** *(https://docs.microsoft.com/en-us/visualstudio/deployment/quickstart-deploy-to-azure?view=vs-2019).*

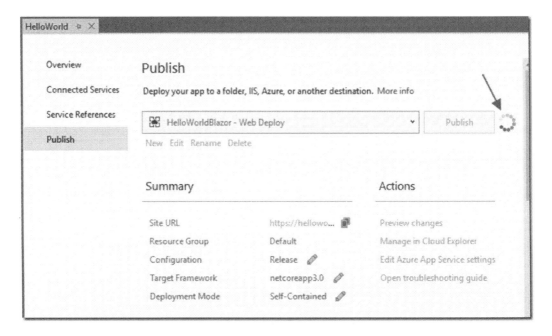

The application will start *deployment...*

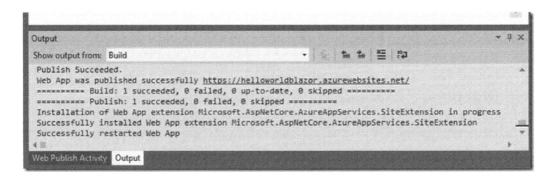

The **output** window will display the progress and indicate when it is done.

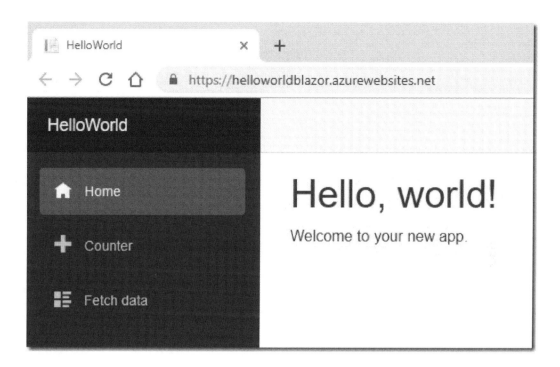

A web browser window will *open* and *display* the deployed application.

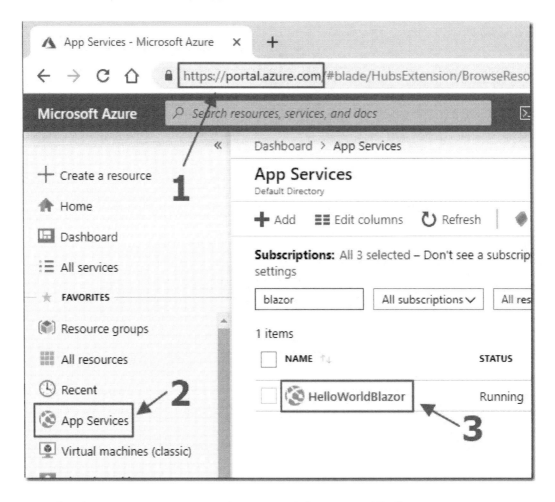

Logging into **Portal.Azure.com** in your web browser will allow you to administer the application.

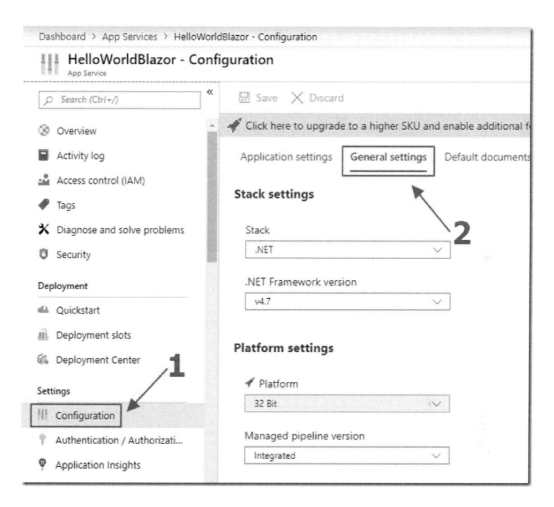

For the best performance, you will want to go into the **Configuration** for your
App Service and select **Configuration** then **General Settings**…

… and turn on **Web sockets** and click **Save**.

You may find that as more users use your **Blazor** application, the response time may slow. However, in many cases it will run fine.

If it does run slow or you have *multiple* **Azure App Service** instances serving a single application, you will want to use an **Azure SignalR Service**.

Create SignalR Service

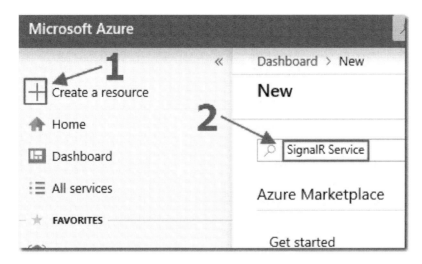

If you do not already have an **Azure SignalR Service**, log into the **Azure Portal**, and select **Create a resource** and search for **SignalR Service**.

Click **Create**.

You can initially choose the **Free** tier.

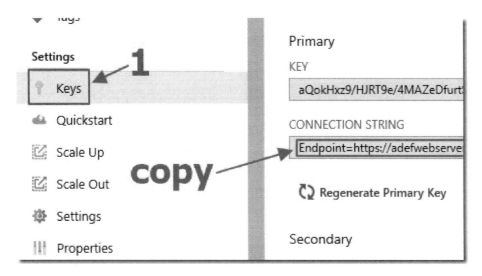

After the service is created, select **Keys**, and copy the **Connection String** (you will need it in the later steps).

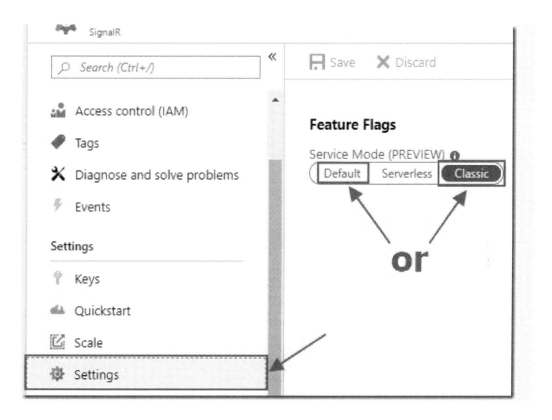

Under **Settings**, set **Service Mode** to either **Default** or **Classic**.

Add SignalR Service

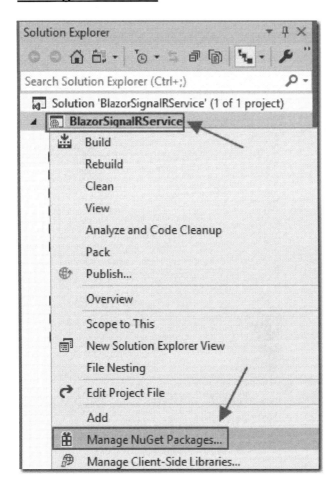

Right-click on the **Solution** node and select **Manage NuGet Packages...**

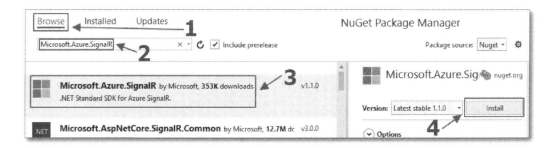

Search for and install **Microsoft.Azure.SignalR**

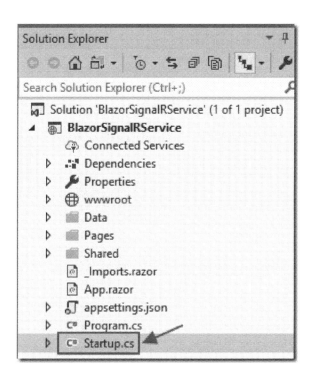

Open the **Startup.cs** file in the **Server** project.

```
public void ConfigureServices(IServiceCollection services)
{
    services.AddSignalR().AddAzureSignalR(
        "{{ Your Azure SignalR Services Connection String }}");
    services.AddRazorPages();
    services.AddServerSideBlazor();
    services.AddSingleton<WeatherForecastService>();
}
```

Change the **ConfigureServices** method to the following:

```
services.AddSignalR().AddAzureSignalR(
    "{{ Your Azure SignalR Services Connection String }}");
```

Note: Replace {{ **Your Azure SignalR Servces Connection String** }} with the connection string you copied earlier.

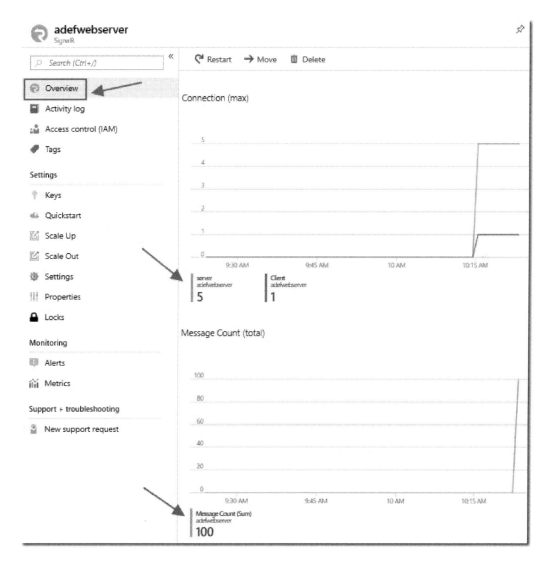

When we run the application and use it, we can look in **Azure** and see the traffic.

Using User Secrets

It is recommended that you don't store the **connection string** in the code.

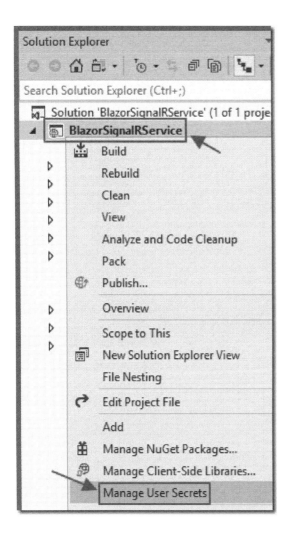

In **Visual Studio,** *right-click* on the project and select **Manage User Secrets.**

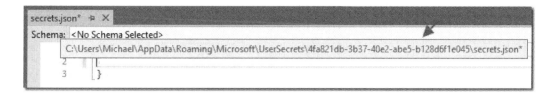

This will open a file called **secrets.json** in a location on your local computer.

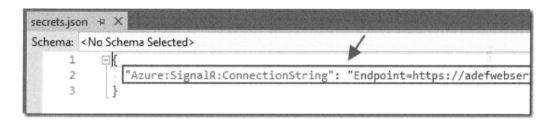

Add a line:

```
"Azure:SignalR:ConnectionString": "{{ Your Azure SignalR Servces Connection String }}"
```

Note: Replace **{{ Your Azure SignalR Servces Connection String }}** with the connection string you copied earlier.

Save and **close** the file.

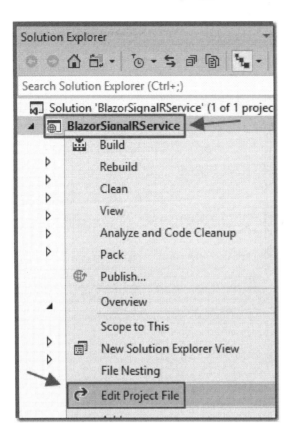

If you now edit the **Project File**…

```
BlazorSignalRService.csproj ⊟ ×
 1 ⊟<Project Sdk="Microsoft.NET.Sdk.Web">
 2
 3 ⊟   <PropertyGroup>
 4        <TargetFramework>netcoreapp3.0</TargetFramework>
 5        <LangVersion>7.3</LangVersion>
 6        <AddRazorSupportForMvc>true</AddRazorSupportForMvc>
 7        <UserSecretsId>4fa821db-3b37-40e2-abe5-b128d6f1e045</UserSecretsId>
 8      </PropertyGroup>
 9
10 ⊟   <ItemGroup>
11        <PackageReference Include="Microsoft.Azure.SignalR" Version="1.1.0-preview1-10404" />
12      </ItemGroup>
13
14    </Project>
15
```

You will now see an entry pointing to the **user secrets file**.

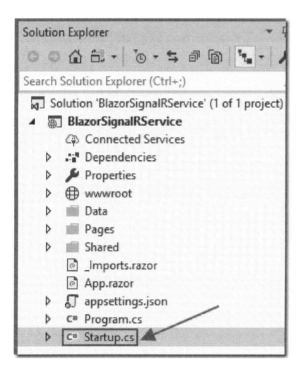

335

An Introduction to Building Applications with Blazor

Open the **Startup.cs** file.

Add the following **using** statement:

```
using Microsoft.Extensions.Configuration;
```

Add the following code to the **Startup** class:

```
public IConfiguration Configuration { get; }
public Startup(IConfiguration configuration)
{
    Configuration = configuration;
}
```

In the **ConfigureServices** method, change the
services.AddSignalR().AddAzureSignalR line to:

```
services.AddSignalR().AddAzureSignalR(Configuration["Azure:SignalR:ConnectionString"]);
```

About the Author

 Michael Washington is an ASP.NET C# programmer. He has extensive knowledge in process improvement, billing systems, and student information systems. He is a Microsoft Reconnect MVP. He has a son, Zachary, and resides in Los Angeles with his wife, Valerie.

He is the author of the following books:

- **ADefHelpDesk 4** (ADefHelpDesk.com)
- **Azure Machine Learning Studio for The Non-Data Scientist** (AiHelpWebsite.com)
- **An Introduction to the Microsoft Bot Framework** (AiHelpWebsite.com)
- **Creating HTML 5 Websites and Cloud Business Apps Using LightSwitch In Visual Studio 2013-2015** (LightSwitchHelpWebsite.com)
- **OData And Visual Studio LightSwitch** (LightSwitchHelpWebsite.com)
- **Building Websites with DotNetNuke 5** (Packt Publishing)

Made in the USA
San Bernardino, CA
10 July 2020